A Critique
of Soviet Economics

A Critique
of Soviet Economics

by Mao Tsetung

Translated by Moss Roberts
Annotated by Richard Levy
With an Introduction
by James Peck

Monthly Review Press
New York and London

Copyright © 1977 by Moss Roberts

Library of Congress Cataloging in Publication Data
Mao, Tsetung, 1893–1976.
   A critique of Soviet economics.
   CONTENTS: Reading notes on the Soviet text *Political
Economy.*—Concerning *Economic Problems of Socialism in
the Soviet Union.*—Critique of Stalin's *Economic
Problems of Socialism in the Soviet Union.*
      1. Economics—Russia.   2. Akademiia nauk SSSR.
Institut ėkonomiki. Politicheskaia ėkonomiia.
3. Stalin, Iosif, 1879–1953. Ėkonomicheskie problemy
sotsializma v SSSR.   4. Russia—Economic policy—
1917–   5. China—Economic policy.   I. Title.
HB113.A2M34213   330'.0947   77-70971
ISBN 0-85345-412-4

Monthly Review Press
62 West 14th Street, New York, N.Y. 10011
47 Red Lion Street, London WC1R 4PF

Manufactured in the United States of America

10 9 8 7 6 5 4 3 2 1

Contents

Introduction

These writings of Mao Tsetung, brought together here under the title *A Critique of Soviet Economics,* date from the period during and immediately after the Great Leap Forward, a time when the Chinese Revolution began to break decisively with the Soviet Union and its model of development. With the Great Leap, a distinctive Chinese road to socialism emerged. But it was a road paved with a decade of controversy over the course of China's socialist development. At the heart of many of those disputes within the Chinese Communist Party was the question of the applicability of the Russian experience to building socialism in China.

In analyzing their own society, the Chinese Communists have long studied the Russian Revolution for inspiration and practical suggestions, as well as for a general perspective on the course of their own revolution. To them, the Soviet Union is a model from which both negative and positive lessons can be drawn. Thus it is not surprising to find Mao, at such a pivotal stage in the Chinese Revolution as the Great Leap, once again turning to a study of Soviet experience. This time he did so through a critique of two Soviet books, *Political Economy: A Textbook* and Joseph Stalin's *Economic Problems of Socialism in the USSR.* By the time Mao wrote his critique, however, he had moved away from trying to adapt Soviet methods, as he and other party leaders had sought to do in the early 1950s, and instead began to advocate strongly a wide range of alternatives.

A Critique of Soviet Economics can usefully be read from several, closely interwoven perspectives: (1) as a crucial initial summing up by Mao of what the Soviet model was and what it implied for China; (2) as a strong defense of the Great Leap Forward from the perspective of uninterrupted revolution; (3) as a pathbreaking examination of the principles of Soviet political economy and of several key aspects of the Russian revolutionary experience, particularly the years under Stalin's leadership.

The texts translated in this volume include a critique of the Soviet work, *Political Economy: A Textbook,* along with a supplement Mao wrote to his own critique, a talk on Stalin's *Economic Problems of Socialism in the USSR,* and a critique of the *Economic Problems of Socialism in the USSR.* Mao's consideration of Stalin's *Economic Problems* together with the Russian political economy text is quite appropriate, as Stalin's work was itself written as a series of comments for the draft textbook on political economy, which was finished and released only after his death. This Russian text in its various Russian/Chinese editions circulated in China from the mid-1950s on. After the Lushan Conference in 1959, Mao called upon party members to critically study the third edition. This was the edition upon which his critique is based.

THE SOVIET MODEL

Throughout most of the history of the Chinese Communist Party, controversy over how to deal with the experience of the Russian Revolution has been at the heart of what the Chinese call the "two-line struggle." From its founding in 1921, conflicts within the party have in one way or another been linked to individuals who favored the orthodox Russian conception of revolution. The defeat of Li Li-san in the 1930s, Wang Ming in the 1940s, Kao Kang (Gau Gang) and P'eng Teh-huai (Peng Deh-huai) in the 1950s, and Liu Shao-ch'i (Liu Shau-qi) in the 1960s have all entailed controversies over the nature and applicability of the Soviet model.

Until 1949, these disputes in China focused on the appropriate strategy and tactics of the revolutionary struggle for power, the nature of the mass line, and the correct way to apply Marxism-Leninism to the concrete conditions of China. Stalin only reluctantly tolerated the methods and innovations associated with Mao and his followers, especially as they were worked out during the years in Yenan (1937–1945). In the 1940s, he even opposed the successful struggle for liberation. "The Chinese revolution won victory," Mao later said, "by acting contrary to Stalin's will. . . . If we had followed Wang Ming's, or in other words, Stalin's, method the Chinese revolution couldn't have succeeded." [1]

With Liberation, however, the Chinese saw the Soviet Union as the model for socialist development. Mao had warned his colleagues in 1949 that "our past work is only the first step in a long march of 10,000 li"—"a brief prologue to a long drama." [2] Yet in these early days, there was no model of socialist development other than the Russian, with its reliance on elite-planned and bureaucratically administered programs of economic development which unduly subordinate the needs of the countryside to the demands of heavy industry. The Soviet Union, despite all, was a society which had achieved industrialization and collectivization, key goals of all the leaders of the Chinese Communist Party. The Soviet victory over fascism in the Second World War was to many Chinese leaders proof of the success of that society. And at a time of intense American government hostility, a U.S.-backed blockade and bombings of its coast, and later a worldwide economic embargo, it was quite natural that China leaned toward the Soviet Union in its defense and economic policies.

"In the early stages of Liberation," Mao writes in this volume, "we had no experience of managing the economy of the entire nation. So in the period of the first five-year plan we could do no more than copy the Soviet Union's methods, although we never felt altogether satisfied about it." [3] This growing dissatisfaction focused around three main aspects of the Soviet model: (1) "primitive socialist accumulation"[4] at the expense of the peasantry; (2) a theory of productive forces and the dictatorship of the proletariat; (3) a conception of the Communist Party in China.

Primitive Socialist Accumulation at the Expense of the Peasantry

A Chinese slogan of the early 1950s, "the Soviet Union today is our tomorrow," captures the spirit with which many Chinese undertook to copy Soviet methods. China's first five-year plan was notable for its almost exclusive reliance on heavy industry; highly centralized, bureaucratic methods of planning; and little emphasis on light industry and the production of consumer goods. The peasantry was considered largely as a source of savings. Powerful, centralized economic ministries were established in Peking. They introduced rigid hierarchical systems of control and "one-man management" in the factories, and relied on highly paid specialists alone to direct them. To stimulate productive activity and monitor enterprise performance, material incentives were widely promoted.

The Soviet Union actively encouraged such developments. And China's relations with the socialist world after 1949 quite naturally entailed giving a priority to those areas where cooperation was easiest and most meaningful: heavy industry, an educational system designed to train professionals and technicians to administer the Soviet-style five-year plan; the spread of professionalization in the armed forces. Indeed, what was happening in the People's Liberation Army symbolizes what was happening throughout the urban areas of China. With the adoption in February 1955 of the "Regulations on the Service of Officers," the Chinese officer corps acquired the trappings of a regular army. And in introducing a system of ranks, titles, and widely divergent pay scales for officers and enlisted personnel, the PLA was turning its back on the informal, egalitarian, and democratic character which had been molded in years of revolutionary warfare.

Opposition to this rapid "Sovietization" was not far below the surface even in these early years after Liberation. Many cadres were uneasy about the party's turning its back on the egalitarian traditions of Yenan. Others, including such leading members as Liu Shao-ch'i, came to oppose the concentration of economic power in the ministries in Peking and the highly centralized planning apparatus which they saw as threatening their conception of the role and authority of the Chinese Communist Party. In subsequent years, as some of the ministries were made less bureaucratic and planning less centralized after the mid-1950s, the party did expand its role. One-man management systems were to give way to greater party involvement in the running of the factories. With the Great Leap Forward, the party also greatly increased its role in the rural areas.

Many party leaders, therefore, were not opposed to some of the criticisms which Mao began to raise about the dangers of copying the Soviet model. Yet for Mao, their criticisms did not go to the heart of the problem. In evaluating the application of the Soviet model in the early 1950s, Mao began to warn of the dangers it posed to the revolutionary transformation of the countryside. The growing gap between town and country, he argued, was reinforcing ingrained habits of looking down on those engaged in manual labor, especially peasants, an attitude that in turn nurtured bureaucratic and elitist methods of leadership. And Mao feared that the growing reliance on industrial and technical development concentrated in the cities at the expense of pushing the social revolution in the countryside would exacerbate the very contradictions that had to be overcome to transform China into an industrialized, socialist society.

In July 1955, Mao insisted that developments in the cities and rural areas were intricately interrelated: "We must on no account regard industry and agriculture, socialist industrialization and the socialist transformation of agriculture as two separate and isolated things, and on no account must we emphasize the one and play down the other."[5] But not until April of 1956, in his speech "On the Ten Major Relationships," did Mao directly challenge the Soviet model's reliance on primitive accumulation at the expense of the peasantry.

Mao sharply criticized the Soviet's "lopsided stress on heavy industry to the neglect of agriculture and light industry."[6] Calling for a reduction in the absolute priority given to heavy industry, he argued that increased investment in light industry and agriculture serves the daily needs of the people while actually speeding up the accumulation of "capital" for heavy industry. To implement this proposal, Mao urged local authorities to take greater initiative, criticizing the Soviet Union for "concentrating everything in the hands of central authorities, shackling the local authorities and denying them the right of independent action."[7] Administrative costs had to be cut, the staff of the national bureaucracies slashed by two-thirds. Unified planning and discipline under a strong center were still essential, he insisted, but this was not the same as the domination of ministries administering a Soviet-style centralization.

In this way, Mao went on to challenge the very basis of the Soviet method of accumulation from the peasantry. The Russians had made "grave mistakes" in handling the peasants and taken measures which "squeeze the peasants very hard." Their methods of accumulation "had seriously dampened the peasants' enthusiasm for production. You want the hen to lay more eggs and yet you don't feed it, you want the horse to run fast and yet you don't let it graze. What kind of logic is this?"[8]

On no account, Mao was saying, would the Chinese follow a development strategy for which the peasants had to pay the cost. Nor could China simply drain the surplus from the rural areas, as Stalin had done in the 1930s. Unlike what both Soviet orthodoxy and bourgeois economists then claimed, the "capital" could not come from any preexisting source of surplus in the rural areas. For precious little "capital" existed. Instead of taking the surplus from the rural areas, therefore, Mao argued that the Chinese labor force, agricultural and industrial alike, had to significantly increase its productivity. In this way, a truly industrialized socialist society could develop. The worker-peasant alliance would be strengthened rather than torn apart by a sharp clash between rural and urban interests. And by avoiding the imposition of a special burden on the peasants, a powerful, repressive state apparatus would not be needed to extract surplus production.

With his speech "On the Ten Major Relationships," as Mao later said, we "made a start in proposing our own line for construction."[9] Mao for the first time clearly rejected the idea of development through a privileged sector (heavy industry, and only later the other sectors) and distinct phases (first in material progress, only later in social relations and ideology). The entire nation, he insisted, must undertake a massive commitment to social, political, and economic unification that, like the methods used in the years in Yenan, would leave none behind and not benefit a few at the expense of the many. In this pathbreaking analysis of the contradictions in China, Mao firmly opposed any plans that would create new divisions in a nation already severely torn by imbalances between the various regions, between various social classes and groups, between the center and the regions, between the political and social spheres.

A Theory of Productive Forces and the Dictatorship of the Proletariat

While pointing out the dangers of blindly copying the Soviet model of accumulation, Mao was also criticizing another, closely associated aspect of that model, its theory of productive forces. Essentially, this theory, as it was formulated in the Soviet Union during the years of Stalin's leadership, maintained that state ownership of the means of production, together with a rapid growth of the forces of production, opens up the socialist road to communism. The dictatorship of the proletariat guides the development of the forces of production, while repressing the old ruling classes and defeating their inevitable counter-revolutionary attacks on the new order.

For the peasants and the workers, the dictatorship of the

proletariat is held to be a genuine democracy. The abolition of private property and other forms of class society is argued to have ended all exploitation. Since exploitation is argued to be impossible under such new conditions, the hierarchy, subordination, and disciplining of the workforce, even when it appears to resemble sophisticated capitalist methods, is seen as merely the adaptation of rational patterns of work.

With the dying out of the old bourgeoisie and feudal ruling classes, the development of the forces of production and the continuous elevation of the standard of living of the masses, class struggle will diminish in intensity and eventually disappear. Were it not for the international struggle with capitalism, the state itself would "wither away." Even though the state does remain as an apparatus to fight external enemies, the transition to communism can be worked out internally, dependent only on the development of the forces of production.

In essence, the Stalinist theory of productive forces reduced the concept of the capitalist mode of production to little more than the system of private ownership of the means of production. And consequently, once political power is seized and a system of public ownership of the means of production instituted, no thought need be given to a thoroughgoing socialist revolution on the political and ideological fronts. The creative role of the masses and mass campaigns are viewed as anachronistic; the struggle to refashion one's worldview is ignored.

Mao's attack on this theory of productive forces grew out of the lessons he had learned about revolutionary transformation during the years of guerrilla warfare.[10] The distinctive features of the Yenan model are well known: self-reliance, decentralization, antagonism to bureaucratism and elitism, collective aims and discipline, nonmaterial incentives, and the participation of the masses in all aspects of social and economic activity. Development was comprehensive, designed to bring up all sectors, not just a chosen part.

Out of the struggles for revolutionary land reform, Mao argued, the peasants' political consciousness had been raised through the mass line and the development of new cooperative work relationships. By changing the relations of production and encouraging the growth of new attitudes and ideas, rural productivity was increased. The party itself was only a part of this process, not its master. For like the peasants, its members were molded through a process of continuous, step-by-step transformation.

Mao's strong advocacy of rapid collectivization in the years after Liberation was predicated upon this experience of developing the productive forces through a step-by-step transformation of every aspect of rural life. Thus he criticized the idea of "mechanization first, cooperation later on," arguing instead that collectivization could and should precede mechanization of agriculture. Social transformation, followed and increasingly supported by technological changes, would release the productive forces while decreasing polarization in the countryside.

Many leading party officials, influenced by the Soviet model's reliance on the theory of primitive accumulation, opposed Mao's call for deepening the rural revolution in the early 1950s. Liu Shao-ch'i reportedly criticized as "utopian agrarian socialism" the attempt to promote cooperativization before there was an adequate supply of agricultural tools and sufficient mechanization. Nor was Liu alone in his doubts. Remembering what had happened in the Soviet Union, many party leaders feared that accelerating collectivization in China would lose them peasant support and disrupt their economic plans. As Mao commented in July 1955:

> some comrades have found in the history of the Communist Party of the Soviet Union grounds for criticizing what they call impetuosity and rashness in our present work of agricultural co-operation . . . but on no account should we allow these comrades to use the Soviet experience as a cover for their idea of moving at a snail's pace.[11]

This debate was not just over the pace of collectivization, however. Mao perceived that behind the opposition to his policies was a more fundamental opposition to continuing class struggle and revolutionary methods of social transformation. In June 1953 he warned party leaders that the transition period to socialism was "filled with contradiction and struggle. Our present revolutionary struggle is even more severe than past armed revolutionary struggle. This is a revolution to bury once and for all capitalism and all exploitative systems."[12]

Yet rather than demonstrating an ability to lead such revolutionary struggle, Mao saw numerous party leaders lagging behind the mass upsurge in the countryside.

> Some of our comrades are tottering along like a woman with bound feet and constantly complaining, "You're going too fast." Excessive criticism, inappropriate complaints, endless anxiety, and the erection of countless taboos—they believe this is the proper way to guide the socialist movement in the rural areas.[13]

If Mao saw the campaign for accelerating collectivization as a testament to the mass line and the need for revolutionary struggle, many party officials argued that successful collectivization set the stage for a new era in which such methods were no longer necessary. Thus even as they began to support Mao's position on primitive accumulation as expressed in "On the Ten Major Relationships," Liu Shao-ch'i and other party leaders concluded that China's collectivization had progressed to a point where the development of the productive forces required that "the principal method of struggle" could no longer be "to lead the masses in direct action."[14] As Liu Shao-ch'i said at the Eighth Party Congress in September 1956:

> Now, however, the period of revolutionary storm and stress is past, new relations of production have been set up, and the aim of our struggle is changed into one of safeguarding the successful development of the productive forces of society, [and thus] a corresponding change in the methods of struggle will consequently have to follow . . .[15]

With the collectivization of agriculture and the public ownership of the means of production basically accomplished by 1956, Liu and others stressed the need to focus all energies on promoting the productive forces. This they did in a way deeply marked by the Soviet model of development. For by maintaining, as the Eighth Party Congress resolution stated, that "the essence of this contradiction [in socialist society] is a contradiction between the advanced social system and the backward social productive forces,"[16] they turned their backs on the need for a simultaneous and interrelated socialist revolution on the political and ideological fronts. Revolutionary struggle, they believed, would not unleash the productive forces, but would only undermine the needed stability for their rapid growth. Periods of acute class struggle were no longer essential to create the new cooperative organizations and attitudes favorable to economic growth. The "advanced social system" already existed and needed only to be consolidated.

In 1956 and 1957, Mao had himself argued that the turbulent class struggles characteristic of previous revolutionary periods had in the main come to an end. But unlike other party leaders, he insisted that "the class struggle between the proletariat and the bourgeoisie, the class struggle between the different political forces, and the class struggle in the ideological field between the proletariat and the bourgeoisie will continue to be long and tortuous and at times will even become very acute."[17] Thus he soon came to reject the Eighth Party Congress resolution that the contradiction in socialist society was between the "advanced social system" and the "backward social productive forces." Rather he argued that

> the basic contradictions in socialist society are still those between the relations of production and the productive forces, and between the superstructure and the economic base . . . survivals of bourgeois ideology, bureaucratic ways of doing things in our state organs, and flaws in certain links of our state institutions stand in contrast to the economic base of socialism.[18]

There were thus serious weaknesses in the "advanced social system" which had to be struggled against. In essence, Mao insisted that only continued mass struggle could combat the powerful hold of bourgeois ideology and bureaucratic ways of doing things. The seizure of state power and the public ownership of the means of production, therefore, were insufficient for the building of socialism. By themselves, they could not consolidate the gains made. The mere growth of the economic base could not automatically engender the very attitudes and organizational forms necessary both to drive the revolution forward and unleash the productive forces of the masses.

In his critique, Mao spells out for his party colleagues what he saw as the long-term consequences of such an exclusive emphasis on building up the economic base. As Mao notes, "in many ways (mainly production) the Soviets continue to progress, but with respect to the production relations fundamentally they have ceased to progress."[19] By resisting revolutionary social changes and not working to transform the basic relations among people in production and society as speedily as possible, the Soviets ensured that no qualitative changes occurred at all. The relations of production were all but frozen. By excluding the creativity and initiative of the masses, the Soviets could not develop the new attitudes and organizational forms necessary for a socialist society and the transition to communism.

Indeed, at the heart of the Soviet theory of productive forces, Mao argued, was a profound fear and distrust of the masses and mass struggle. This was what the Soviet political economy text and Stalin's *Economic Problems of Socialism* revealed in their preoccupation with the base at the expense of the superstructure. For Mao, a host of closely related Soviet positions flowed from this preoccupation: disregard for the masses as the creators of history and a reliance on planners; preoccupation with technology and expertise; confidence in hierarchy and one-man management; reliance on material incentives; and a total lack of interest in the transformation of an individual's worldview. The end result was the growth of a powerful bureaucratic apparatus completely alienated from the masses.

A Conception of the Communist Party

Mao's denunciation of such bureaucratic ways ran throughout his entire revolutionary career. But with the seizure of state power Mao faced questions for which he found no answers in Soviet revolutionary experience. How, for example, was the party to retain its intimate ties with the masses when the tendency toward bureaucratic methods and elite privilege was so powerful? How was the revolution to be continued after state power was seized and the means of production brought under public ownership?

Khrushchev's attack on Stalin in February 1956 pointedly raised such questions for Mao and other party leaders. Although the Chinese Communist Party sharply criticized Khrushchev's lack of a cogent theoretical perspective for evaluating Stalin, at the same time the dangers of Stalinism were not dismissed. In the first official Chinese Communist Party response in April 1956, the party strongly reaffirmed the mass line and warned of the dangers of its neglect when a communist party was in power:

> the personnel of the Party and the state, beset by bureaucratism from many sides, face the great danger of using the machinery of state to take arbitrary action, alienating themselves from the masses and collective leadership, resorting to commandism, and violating Party and state democracy.[20]

As Mao argued in "On the Correct Handling of Contradictions Among the People," there are "contradictions between the government and the people in socialist countries."[21] By always talking about unity and consolidation, the Soviet Union was actually blocking the correct resolution of the various contradictions in society, impeding the development of socialism. The real problems facing society remained hidden. And a convenient ideological cover for bureaucratic domination was created.

But while various party leaders warned of the dangers of bureaucracy and spoke of the mass line, there were very pronounced differences in how they understood them and the role of the Communist Party. Liu Shao-ch'i was often labeled in the Chinese press during the Cultural Revolution as the main ideological critic of Mao's views on the mass line. If so, he assuredly had significant support for his views; his position in many ways followed the conception of the Communist Party as it was enshrined in official Soviet doctrine. For Liu, the party, and only the party, could see what was necessary and could see to these necessary changes. To the masses, it would appear as a united, selflessly dedicated organization. Purity of devotion and ideological orthodoxy were the ultimate safeguards for the ability of the party to act correctly on behalf of the masses. Only after its members had been taught "how to be good communists" could the party effectively help the masses to solve their problems. A selfless party elite should thus be above external supervision; its mistakes could be satisfactorily rectified through intraparty channels. As Mao said in the fall of 1957, "Some seem to think that once in the Communist Party, people all become saints with no differences or misunderstandings, and that the Party is not subject to analysis, that is to say, it is monolithic and uniform. . . ."[22]

At the heart of Mao's disagreement with Liu's orthodox conception of the Communist Party was his insistence that the party itself is only an instrument involved in, but not dominating, the dialectical process of continuous revolution. Knowledge, he points out in the critique, is not first the exclusive domain of the party elite. The party does not stand outside the revolutionary process with foreknowledge of its laws. "For people to know the laws they must go through a process. The vanguard is no exception."[23] Only through practice can knowledge develop; only by immersing itself among the masses can the party lead the revolution.

Throughout the history of the Chinese Revolution, Mao criticized those who believed they knew exactly what had to be done and relied on Marxism-Leninism as an abstract doctrine filled with ready-made answers. Revolution, Mao insisted, is an extraordinarily painful and difficult process.

There are no easy answers, no laws which can be simply applied. As he argues in the critique, years of arduous struggle had been necessary before the correct methods emerged to enable the Chinese revolutionaries to win the bourgeois-democratic phase of the revolution. The building of socialism and communism would require an equally arduous struggle.

Mao saw the masses as the real creators of history, those from whom the Communist Party had to learn. Mistakes and setbacks would emerge in any mass struggle; revolution is sometimes brutal and violent. But the creative breakthroughs which lead to new cooperative methods and attitudes only come out of revolutionary struggle. This was how the soviets had emerged in the Russian Revolution, Mao maintained, and how the communes developed in China. Nor should one fear failures. "People must go through practice to gain results, meet with failures as problems arise; only through such a process can knowledge gradually advance."[24] Failures, correctly analyzed, are often as illuminating as successes. By studying those which occurred in the Great Leap Forward, for example, Mao sought to uncover the guidelines within which consolidation of the communes could be accomplished.

No leadership, in short, can create the new social forms and political and economic innovations out of its own heads, then apply them through administrative decree. New forms and methods will emerge, Mao insisted, if cadres and the masses are allowed to experiment, if they are mobilized and encouraged by a party leadership willing to learn from their potential breakthroughs and capable of both shaping and being shaped in the process. As Mao said during the period of accelerating collectivization in 1955: "Both cadres and peasants will remold themselves in the course of the struggles they themselves experience. Let them go into action and learn while doing, and they will become more capable."[25]

Unlike Liu Shao-ch'i, therefore, Mao never saw ideological devotion and intraparty rectification movements as sufficient to maintain the revolutionary role of the party. Only by being immersed in the masses, subject to their criticism, and

sensitive to their needs could the party truly combat bureaucracy, privilege, and elitism. And since for him the party did
not stand above society, Mao came to see the contradictions
within the party as intricately interwoven with those in the
society at large. In his editing of *Socialist Upsurge in China's
Countryside* in 1955, Mao first mentioned the theme which
he was to raise in the critique and elaborate further in later
years. There is a practice, he then warned, "prevalent almost
to the point of being universal: right opportunists in the
party, working hand in glove with the forces of capitalism in
society, are preventing the broad masses of poor and middle
peasants from taking the road to the formation of cooperatives."[26] This emphasis on rightists in the party linked to social forces was to undercut further the orthodox Soviet conception of the party and was used in the coming years as
another reason for deepening the mass-line conception of
politics.

THE GREAT LEAP FORWARD

Mao's writings in this volume can also be read as an analysis
of the Great Leap Forward. Here for the first time in his
known writings, Mao is extensively exploring the process of
uninterrupted revolution and the nature of the transition to
socialist and communist society.[27] In so doing, he defends
the Great Leap against unfounded attacks both from within
and outside the party. At the same time, he is seeking to
elaborate the context within which the Great Leap's negative
features can be corrected and its positive aspects preserved.

These writings can be read for the fine insight they give
into the way Mao understood his own methods of study. He
does not start from rules, principles, Marxist laws, or assumed definitions, "a methodology Marxism-Leninism has
always opposed."[28] Only through concrete investigation can
new principles be discovered. Indeed, one of his strongest
criticisms of Stalin and the Soviet political economy text is
that "it does not proceed from concrete analysis of the con-

tradictions between the economic base and the superstructure. It always proceeds from general definitions and general conceptions. It gives definitions without giving reasoned explanations."[29]

Thus, Mao studies Stalin's *Economic Problems of Socialism* in order to think through specific practical and theoretical problems facing China, in this case the creation of the communes. With their creation as a new unit in society, analysis of how production and exchange should be carried out within and between communes and other units was a pressing necessity. Therefore, Mao's comments are largely focused on the first three sections of *Economic Problems of Socialism,* those concerned with the character of economic laws, commodity production, and the law of value under socialism. What Mao finds useful in Stalin's writings is carefully separated from what he concludes is unclear or inaccurate.

Mao argues that one of the most useful reasons for having the cadres read Stalin's *Economic Problems of Socialism* is to enable them to understand the ultra-left current (the "communist wind") which had quickly spread over China with the beginning of the commune movement. As Mao later said at the Lushan Conference in July 1959, the cadres

> had not studied political economy. They had not clearly understood the laws of value, exchange of equal values, and remuneration according to work done. . . . If they have not understood the textbooks, let them study them some more. If the top cadres in the communes do not understand a little political economy, this won't do.[30]

To Mao, a better understanding of the economics of socialism and the nature of the transition period would allow the cadres to cope with the problems arising in the Great Leap. In some areas, both cadres and peasants had been swept away by a desire to leap directly to the stage of communism rather than going through the many stages that Mao argued were necessary to get there. The "strong tendency to do away with commodity production" had to be countered and its role in socialist society correctly understood. "People get upset the minute they see commodity production," Mao writes in his critique, "taking it for capitalism. But it looks as if commodity production will have to be greatly developed and the money supply increased." And explaining this "poses a problem for the ideology of several hundred thousand cadres as well as for the solidarity of several hundred million peasants."[31]

In some areas of China, the cadres, in their impassioned desire to leap to communism, had simply seized the property of the production brigades and the teams. Were such practices to go unchecked, Mao warned, the peasants would rise up and turn their wrath on the Communist Party itself. Study of Stalin's *Economic Problems of Socialism,* because it defends the survival of the commodity form into the socialist period and discusses the principle of exchange of equal value, could help provide theoretical guidance against this dangerous ultra-left current.

In his critique of the Soviet political economy text, Mao further examined the lessons to be drawn from the Great Leap. He studied the relationships that exist between the two kinds of ownership of the means of production (socialist ownership by the whole people and collective ownership, largely by the peasants) and compared them with those which existed in the Soviet Union. The abortive attempt to immediately make the commune rather than the production team the basic accounting unit is examined. Questions of distribution of consumer goods are probed in terms of why the principle of "from each according to his ability, to each according to his work" is still necessary during the stages of socialism. Mao, in brief, is working out the consequences of the use of the commodity system, exchange through money, and bourgeois right, particularly as they are reflected in the three major differences: between workers and peasants, between town and country, and between mental and manual labor.

Running through all his comments is the argument that Soviet experience is in the final analysis utterly inadequate as a positive model for China's drive to build socialism. The political economy text, Mao concludes, does not satisfactorily cope with the "whole new series of problems" that have appeared with the period of socialism. It does not suggest how to move from one stage of the revolution to another, or the special characteristics of each stage. For example, he argues, it fails to consider how to advance the process of the transformation of the small producers, what kinds of contradictions may be found in each stage of the transformation, and how they can be resolved. Indeed, the text speaks of "consolidating fully" each and every stage. Rather than becoming a transient goal which is to be surpassed once it is partially achieved (and thus truly consolidated), the stage becomes an end in itself. In this way, Mao concludes, the Russians simply repressed all consideration of a continuing revolutionary process on the economic, political, and ideological fronts.

Mao's writings in this critique are transitional documents: they stand midway on the path to the Great Proletarian Cultural Revolution. As Mao's criticism of the Soviet model of socialism deepened during the Great Leap, so did his conviction that the transition to socialism was an arduous, protracted struggle that might take an entire historical epoch. Like Lenin, Mao became increasingly concerned with the obstacles and difficulties in this transition. The drive toward socialism requires that every aspect of society undergo tremendous change. In this critique, Mao writes of those forces fighting tenaciously to resist such change, calling them "conservative forces" and "rightists." But Mao is still working out the nature of such opposition and its relationship to the Communist Party; he is not stating it precisely. Nor is he saying precisely what is meant by class struggle during the period of socialist transition. Old bourgeois and feudal elements remain in Chinese society, but it is the hold of old values, ideas, and habits of thought which increasingly concerns him. These writings also demonstrate his efforts to challenge those in the party in positions of authority, the managers, technicians, administrators, and other assorted experts who, compared to the workers and peasants, occupy positions of financial reward and power. He finds the children of the cadres disappointing, too protected and with too many political airs. But the dangers to the revolution are still seen in terms of spreading bureaucratism rather than a question of class. This is particularly evident in Mao's cautious explanation of the bureaucratic nature of the Soviet Union and in his lack of a complete study of the material base of the bureaucracy's privileged role. Not until July 1964, in "On Khrushchev's Phoney Communism and Its Historical Lessons for the World," did Mao state that "the contradiction between the Soviet people and this privileged stratum is now the principal contradiction inside the Soviet Union and it is an irreconcilable and antagonistic class contradiction."[32]

The struggles with those in China who opposed the Great Leap Forward forced Mao to deepen the analysis of his critics. Out of this attack on the Great Leap Forward, led first by P'eng Teh-huai and continued by others in the coming years, Mao was to elaborate his conception of "continuing the revolution under the dictatorship of the proletariat." Not until 1962, however, would rightists within the party be labeled revisionists. And not until the Cultural Revolution would the conception of the "capitalist roader" be developed.

STALIN AND THE RUSSIAN REVOLUTION

A Critique of Soviet Economics is quite suggestive for reevaluating the Russian Revolution and the role of Stalin. Although these pieces can usefully be read from this perspective, they were not written by Mao as a historical study or even as a critical evaluation of the historic contribution of Stalin. Mao's real purpose was to think through problems facing the Chinese Revolution in terms of the perspective offered by a careful examination of aspects of the Soviet experience.

Although these writings were circulated for inner party discussion in China during the Cultural Revolution, they have never been made officially available. The Chinese preface to these materials warns that they may not be fully accurate and complete. Yet even so, they are on the whole quite accurate and provide a remarkably valuable and detailed analysis of Stalin and the Soviet experience, the likes of which have never been publicly available in China.

Officially, the Chinese have for the most part defended Stalin since Khrushchev's attack on him. "When Stalin was criticized in 1956," Mao said, "we were on the one hand happy, but on the other hand apprehensive. It was completely necessary to remove the lid, to break down blind faith, to release the pressure, and to emancipate thought. But we did not agree with demolishing him at one blow."[33]

Publicly, Stalin is seen as a "great Marxist-Leninist" who inherited the cause of Lenin, led the Soviet people in achieving socialist industrialization, agricultural collectivization, and victory in the struggle against fascism. But he is acknowledged to have made serious mistakes. Over the last two decades these have been said to include the following: departing from Marxist-Leninist dialectics in his understanding of the laws of class struggle in socialist society; failing to recognize that after the collectivization of agriculture antagonistic class struggle and the contradiction between the socialist and capitalist roads would continue; failing to rely upon the working class and the masses in the struggle against the forces of capitalism and reducing the threat of capitalist restoration to one of armed attack from international imperialism; seriously neglecting agriculture and peasant living standards and lopsidedly stressing heavy industry; lacking vigilance before the German attack on the Soviet Union; excessively widening the scope of suppression of counterrevolutionaries in the purges of the 1930s.

Mao's criticisms of Stalin in this book go to the very heart of the methods used to industrialize the Soviet Union. Because of this, they provide an important Marxist analysis of the Soviet Union which in the future may well be integrated into official Chinese views, even as they should now contribute to a Marxist understanding of the Soviet Union which is developing outside China.

—James Peck

Notes

1. Mao Tsetung, "Talks at the Chengtu Conference, Talk of March 10, 1958," in *Chairman Mao Talks to the People: Talks and Letters, 1956–1971,* ed. Stuart Schram (New York: Pantheon, 1974), p. 102.
2. Mao Tsetung, *Selected Works of Mao Tsetung,* vol. IV (Peking: Foreign Languages Press, 1965), pp. 422 and 374.
3. Mao Tsetung, *A Critique of Soviet Economics,* p. 122.
4. "Primitive socialist accumulation" was a phrase used by Evgeny Preobrazhensky but it appropriately describes Stalin's policies. See Paul Sweezy's use of the phrase and his analysis in "Theory and Practice in the Mao Period," *Monthly Review* 28, no. 9 (February 1977): 1–12. Sweezy's explanation of the theory of productive forces in the Soviet Union has been drawn upon extensively in this introduction.
5. Mao Tsetung, "On the Question of Agricultural Co-operation," in *Selected Readings from the Works of Mao Tsetung* (Peking: Foreign Languages Press, 1971), p. 406.
6. Mao Tsetung, "On the Ten Major Relationships," *Peking Review* 20, no. 1 (January 1, 1977): 11. Although various unofficial versions of this speech have long been available, this version is the first officially released one.
7. Ibid., p. 16.
8. Ibid., p. 15.
9. Mao Tsetung, "Talks at the Chengtu Conference," p. 101.
10. John G. Gurley, *China's Economy and the Maoist Strategy* (New York: Monthly Review Press, 1976) provides a valuable analysis of the formation of Mao's economic strategy from 1927 to 1949.
11. Mao Tsetung, "On the Question of Agricultural Co-operation," p. 407.
12. Mao Tsetung, "Refute Right Deviationist Views that Depart from the General Line," *Selected Works of Mao Tsetung,* vol. V (Peking: Chinese Language Press, 1977). Translated from the Chinese.
13. Mao Tsetung, "On the Question of Agricultural Co-operation," p. 389.
14. Liu Shao-chi, "The Political Report of the Central Committee of the Communist Party of China to the Eighth National Congress of the Party," in *Eighth National Congress of the Communist Party of China,* vol. 1, Documents (Peking: Foreign Languages Press, 1956), p. 82.

15. Ibid.
16. "Resolution of the Eighth National Congress of the Communist Party of China," in *Eighth National Congress of the Communist Party*, p. 116.
17. Mao Tsetung, "On the Correct Handling of Contradictions Among the People," in *Selected Readings from the Works of Mao Tsetung*, p. 463.
18. Ibid., pp. 443–44.
19. Mao Tsetung, *A Critique of Soviet Economics*, p. 101.
20. Chinese Communist Party, *The Historical Experience of the Dictatorship of the Proletariat* (Peking: Foreign Languages Press, 1959).
21. Mao Tsetung, "On the Correct Handling of Contradictions Among the People," p. 434.
22. Mao Tsetung, "A Dialectical Approach to Inner-Party Unity," in *Selected Works of Mao Tsetung*, vol. V (Peking: Foreign Languages Press, 1977), p. 515.
23. Mao Tsetung, *A Critique of Soviet Economics*, p. 73.
24. Ibid., p. 72.
25. Mao Tsetung, "On the Question of Agricultural Co-operation," p. 390.
26. Mao Tsetung, *Socialist Upsurge in China's Countryside* (Peking: Foreign Languages Press, 1957), p. 159.
27. For a development of the theme of uninterrupted revolution see Victor Nee and James Peck, *China's Uninterrupted Revolution* (New York: Pantheon, 1975).
28. Mao Tsetung, *A Critique of Soviet Economics*, pp. 73–74.
29. Ibid., p. 108.
30. Mao Tsetung, "Speech at the Lushan Conference," in Schram, *Chairman Mao Talks*, pp. 135–36.
31. Mao Tsetung, *A Critique of Soviet Economics*, p. 140.
32. "On Khrushchev's Phoney Communism and Its Historical Lessons for the World: Comment on the Open Letter of the Central Committee of the CPSU (#9)" in *Peking Review* 7, no. 29 (July 17, 1964).
33. Mao Tsetung, "Talks at Chengtu: On the Problem of Stalin," in Schram, *Chairman Mao Talks*, p. 101.

Notes on the Texts

These writings by Mao Tsetung are part of a larger body of materials, entitled *Long Live the Thought of Mao Tsetung,* which appeared first in 1967 and again in an enlarged form in 1969. All three of the works translated here are in the 1969 edition, and the first two are also in the 1967 edition. This means that there are two editions of the *Reading Notes on the Soviet Text Political Economy* and the talk on *Economic Problems of Socialism in the USSR*.

The two versions agree almost entirely, but there are a few differences—some typographical, some substantive. The substantive ones are indicated in footnotes to the translation.[1] Unless otherwise noted, the 1969 version is used when there are minor stylistic differences between the two versions.

Mao's talk on *Economic Problems of Socialism in the USSR* was probably given at the Ch'engchou Conference in November 1958, while his written critique was done in 1959. The 1967 version of *Long Live the Thought of Mao Tsetung* gives the date of the *Reading Notes* as 1960; the 1969 edition gives 1961–1962. We believe that the date of the *Reading Notes* is almost certainly 1960.

The prefaces to these two collections warn that the materials are not for formal publication. Nothing more than speculation exists as to who released the materials and with what intention. We believe the Chinese text we have used is a copy of the original version which probably left China through Taiwan or Hong Kong conduits.

Certain possible limitations to the translation of the *Reading Notes* should be mentioned. The page references Mao cites in making his critique are to the third Chinese edition of the Soviet textbook, and no reference to the original Russian text was made. We had no access to this Chinese edition so that Mao's quotations from the original could not be checked against their source and compared with the Russian.

Although a phonetic transliteration system, Pin-yin, is increasingly widely used in China as the method of romanizing Chinese characters, we have used the modified Wade-Giles system in the text because it is still the one recognized by most Westerners. In both the Introduction and the Notes, however, we have included the new forms in parentheses for interested readers. For those names that appear in the text, for which this procedure was too cumbersome, a representative table of equivalents is provided below.

Wade-Giles	*Pin-yin*
Honan	Henan
Hopei	Hebei
Ch'engchou	Chengzhou
Ch'engtu	Chengdu
Kuangtung	Guangdong
Sinkiang	Xinjiang
Ch'inghai	Qinghai
Fukien	Fujian
Ninghsia	Ningxia
Chihlo	Zhilo
Shaokuan	Shaoguan
Chekiang	Zhejiang
Hsiuwu	Xiuwu

Finally, a comment on the making of *A Critique of Soviet Economics*. Moss Roberts translated the texts, while Richard Levy checked the translation and made many corrections. James Peck and Paul Sweezy read the translation and offered additional suggestions. The introduction was written by James Peck, but it owes much to the criticisms and suggestions of Richard Levy and Moss Roberts. The annotations were written by Richard Levy and edited by James Peck and Moss Roberts. Finally, those of us involved in this project wish to give a special thanks to Karen Judd for her editorial assistance, patience, and good cheer.

Notes
1. For an analysis of the substantive differences between the two editions of *Long Live the Thought of Mao Tsetung,* the dating of the writings translated here, and a study of the writings themselves, see Richard Levy, "New Light on Mao," *The China Quarterly* 61 (1975).

Reading Notes on the Soviet Text *Political Economy* (1961-1962)

PART I: CHAPTERS 20–23

1. *From Capitalism to Socialism*

The text says on pages 327–28 that socialism will "inevitably" supersede capitalism and moreover will do so by "revolutionary means." In the imperialist period clashes between the productive forces and the production relations have become sharper than ever. The proletarian socialist revolution is an "objective necessity." Such statements are quite satisfactory and should be made this way. "Objective necessity" is quite all right and is agreeable to people. To call the revolution an objective necessity simply means that the direction it takes does not hinge on the intentions of individuals. Like it or not, come it will.

The proletariat will "organize all working people around itself for the purpose of eliminating capitalism." (p. 327) Correct. But at this point one should go on to raise the question of the seizure of power. "The proletarian revolution cannot hope to come upon ready-made socialist economic forms." "Components of a socialist economy cannot mature inside of a capitalist economy based on private ownership." (p. 328) Indeed, not only can they not "mature"; they cannot be born. In capitalist societies a cooperative or state-run economy cannot even be brought into being, to say nothing of maturing. This is our main difference with the revisionists, who claim that in capitalist societies such things as municipal public enterprises are actually socialist elements, and argue that capitalism may peacefully grow over to socialism. This is a serious distortion of Marxism.

2. *The Transition Period*

The book says, "The transition period begins with the establishment of proletarian political power and ends with the fulfillment of the responsibility of the socialist revolution—the founding of socialism, communism's first stage." (p. 328) One must study very carefully what stages, in the final analysis, are included in the transition period. Is only the transition from capitalism to socialism included, or the transition from socialism to communism as well?

Here Marx is cited: from capitalism to communism there is a "period of revolutionary transformation." We are presently in such a period. Within a certain number of years our people's communes will have to carry through the transformation from ownership by the basic team to ownership by the basic commune,[1] and then into ownership by the whole people.[2] The transformation to basic commune ownership already carried out by the people's communes remains collective ownership [and is not yet ownership by the whole people].*

In the transition period "all social relations must be fundamentally transformed." This proposition is correct in principle. All social relations includes in its meaning the production relations and the superstructure—economics, politics, ideology and culture, etc.

In the transition period we must "enable the productive forces to gain the development they need to guarantee the victory of socialism." For China, broadly speaking, I would say we need 100–200 million tons of steel per year at the least. Up to this year our main accomplishment has been to clear the way for the development of the productive forces. The de-

---

* Bracketed material has been inserted for clarity by the translator.

velopment of the productive forces of China's socialism has barely begun. Having gone through the Great Leap Forward of 1958–1959, we can look to 1960 as a year promising great development of production.

3. Universal and Particular Characteristics of the Proletarian Revolution in Various Countries

The book says, the October Revolution "planted the standard," and that every country "has its own particular forms and concrete methods for constructing socialism." This proposition is sound. In 1848 there was a Communist Manifesto. One hundred and ten years later there was another Communist Manifesto, namely the Moscow Declaration made in 1957 by various communist parties. This declaration addressed itself to the integration of universal laws and concrete particulars.

To acknowledge the standard of the October Revolution is to acknowledge that the "basic content" of the proletarian revolution of any country is the same. Precisely here we stand opposed to the revisionists.

Why was it that the revolution succeeded first not in the nations of the West with a high level of capitalist productivity and a numerous proletariat, but rather in the nations of the East, Russia and China for example, where the level of capitalist productivity was comparatively low and the proletariat comparatively small? This question awaits study.

Why did the proletariat win its first victory in Russia? The text says because "all the contradictions of imperialism came together in Russia." The history of revolution suggests that the focal point of the revolution has been shifting from West to East. At the end of the eighteenth century the focal point was in France, which became the center of the political life of the world. In the mid-nineteenth century the focal point shifted to Germany, where the proletariat stepped onto the political stage, giving birth to Marxism. In the early years of the twentieth century the focal point shifted to Russia, giving birth to Leninism. Without this development of Marxism there would have been no victory for the Russian Revolution. By the mid-twentieth century the focal point of world revolution had shifted to China. Needless to say, the focal point is bound to shift again in the future.

Another reason for the victory of the Russian Revolution was that broad masses of the peasantry served as an allied force of the revolution. The text says, "The Russian proletariat formed an alliance with the poor* peasants." (p. 328–29, 1967 edition) Among the peasants there are several strata, and the poor peasant is the one the proletariat relied on. When a revolution begins the middle peasants always waver; they want to look things over and see whether the revolution has any strength, whether it can maintain itself, whether it will have advantages to offer. But the middle peasant will not shift over to the side of the proletariat until he has a comparatively clear picture. That is how the October Revolution was. And that is how it was for our own land reform, cooperatives, and people's communes.[3]

Ideologically, politically, and organizationally the Bolshevik-Menshevik split prepared the way for the victory of the October Revolution. And without the Bolsheviks' struggle against the Mensheviks and the revisionism of the Second International, the October Revolution could never have triumphed. Leninism was born and developed in the struggle against all forms of revisionism and opportunism. And without Leninism there would have been no victory for the Russian Revolution.

The book says, "Proletarian revolution first succeeded in Russia, and prerevolutionary Russia had a level of capitalist development sufficient to enable the revolution to succeed." The victory of the proletarian revolution may not have to come in a country with a high level of capitalist development. The book is quite correct to quote Lenin. Down to the present time, of the countries where socialist revolution has succeeded only East Germany and Czechoslovakia had a

---

* Only in the 1969 text.

comparatively high level of capitalism; elsewhere the level was comparatively low. And revolution has not broken out in any of the Western nations with a comparatively high level of development. Lenin had said, "The revolution first breaks out in the weak link of the imperialist world." At the time of the October Revolution Russia was such a weak link. The same was true for China after the October Revolution. Both Russia and China had a relatively numerous proletariat and a vast peasantry, oppressed and suffering. And both were large states. . . .* But in these respects India was much the same. The question is, why could not India consummate a revolution by breaking imperialism's weak link as Lenin and Stalin had described? Because India was an English colony, a colony belonging to a single imperialist state. Herein lies the difference between India and China. China was a semicolony under several imperialist governments. The Indian Communist Party did not take an active part in its country's bourgeois democratic revolution and did not make it possible for the Indian proletariat to assume the leadership of the democratic revolution. Nor, after independence, did the Indian Communist Party persevere in the cause of the independence of the Indian proletariat.

The historical experience of China and Russia proves that to win the revolution having a mature party is a most important condition. In Russia the Bolsheviks took an active part in the democratic revolution and proposed a program for the 1905 revolution distinct from that of the bourgeoisie. It was a program that aimed to solve not only the question of overthrowing the tsar, but also the question of how to wrest leadership from the Constitutional Democratic Party in the struggle to overthrow the tsar.

At the time of the 1911 revolution China still had no communist party. After it was founded in 1921, the Chinese Communist Party immediately and energetically joined the democratic revolution and stood at its forefront. The golden age of China's bourgeoisie, when their revolution had great

---

* Ellipsis in original.

vitality, was during the years 1905–1917. After the 1911 revolution the Nationalist Party was already declining. And by
1924 they had no alternative but to turn to the Communist
Party before they could make further headway. The proletariat had superseded the bourgeoisie. The proletarian political
party superseded the bourgeois political party as the leader of
the democratic revolution. We have often said that in 1927
the Chinese Communist Party had not yet reached its matu-
rity. Primarily this means that our party, during its years of
alliance with the bourgeoisie, failed to see the possibility of
the bourgeoisie betraying the revolution and, indeed, was utterly unprepared for it.

Here (p. 331) the text goes on to express the view that
the reason why countries dominated by precapitalist economic forms could carry through a socialist revolution was
because of assistance from advanced socialist countries. This
is an incomplete way of putting the matter. After the democratic revolution succeeded in China we were able to take the
path of socialism mainly because we overthrew the rule of
imperialism, feudalism, and bureaucratic capitalism. The internal factors were the main ones. While the assistance we
received from successful socialist countries was an important
condition, it was not one which could settle the question of
whether or not we could take the road of socialism, but only
one which could influence our rate of advance after we had
taken the road. With aid we could advance more quickly,
without it less so. What we mean by assistance includes, in
addition to economic aid, our studious application of the positive and negative experiences of both the successes and the
failures of the assisting country.

4. The Question of "Peaceful Transition"

The book says on page 330, "In certain capitalist countries
and former colonial countries, for the working class to take
political power through peaceful parliamentary means is a
practical possibility." Tell me, which are these "certain coun-

tries"? The main capitalist countries of Europe and North America are armed to the teeth. Do you expect them to allow you to take power peacefully?

The communist party and the revolutionary forces of every country must ready both hands, one for winning victory peacefully, one for taking power with violence. Neither may be dispensed with. It is essential to realize that, considering the general trend of things, the bourgeoisie has no intention of relinquishing its political power. They will put up a fight for it, and if their very life should be at stake, why should they not resort to force? In the October Revolution as in our own, both hands were ready. Before July 1917 Lenin did consider using peaceful methods to win the victory, but the July incident demonstrated that it would no longer be possible to transfer power to the proletariat peacefully. And not until he had reversed himself and carried out three months' military preparation did he win the victory of the October Revolution. After the proletariat had seized political power in the course of the October Revolution Lenin remained inclined toward peaceful methods, using "redemption" to eliminate capitalism and put the socialist transformation into effect. But the bourgeoisie in collusion with fourteen imperialist powers launched counter-revolutionary armed uprisings and interventions. And so before the victory of the October Revolution could be consolidated, three years of armed struggle had to be waged under the leadership of the Russian party.

---

5. From the Democratic Revolution to the Socialist Revolution—Several Problems

---

At the end of page 330 the text takes up the transformation of the democratic revolution into the socialist revolution but does not clearly explain how the transformation is effected. The October Revolution was a socialist revolution which concomitantly fulfilled tasks left over from the bourgeois democratic revolution. Immediately after the victory of the October

Revolution the nationalization of land was proclaimed. But
bringing the democratic revolution to a conclusion on the
land question was yet to take a period of time.

During the War of Liberation China solved the tasks of
the democratic revolution. The founding of the People's Republic of China in 1949 marked the basic conclusion of the
democratic revolution and the beginning of the transition to
socialism. It took another three years to conclude the land
reform, but at the time the Republic was founded we immediately expropriated the bureaucratic capitalist enterprises—
80 percent of the fixed assets of our industry and transport—and converted them to ownership by the whole people.

During the War of Liberation we raised antibureaucratic
capitalist slogans as well as anti-imperialist and antifeudal
ones. The struggle against bureaucratic capitalism had a two-
sided character: it had a democratic revolutionary character
insofar as it amounted to opposition to compradore capitalism,[4] but it had a socialist character insofar as it amounted to
opposition to the big bourgeoisie.

After the war of resistance was won, the Nationalist Party
[KMT] took over a very large portion of bureaucratic capital
from Japan and Germany and Italy. The ratio of bureaucratic
to national [i.e., Chinese] capital was 8 to 2. After liberation
we expropriated all bureaucratic capital, thus eliminating the
major components of Chinese capitalism.[5]

But it would be wrong to think that after the liberation of
the whole country "the revolution in its earliest stages had
only in the main the character of a bourgeois democratic revolution and not until later would it gradually develop into a
socialist revolution." [No page reference]

6. Violence and the Proletarian Dictatorship

On page 333 the text could be more precise in its use of the
concept of violence. Marx and Engels always said that "the
state is by definition an instrument of violence employed to
suppress the opposing class." And so it can never be said that

"the proletarian dictatorship does not use violence purely and simply in dealing with the exploiter and may even not use it primarily."

When its life is at stake the exploiting class always resorts to force. Indeed, no sooner do they see the revolution start up than they suppress it with force. The text says, "Historical experience proves that the exploiting class is utterly unwilling to cede political power to the people and uses armed force to oppose the people's political power." This is not a complete way of stating the matter. It is not only after the people have organized revolutionary political power that the exploiting class will oppose it with force, but even at the very moment when the people rise up to seize political power, the exploiters promptly use violence to suppress the revolutionary people.

The purpose of our revolution is to develop the society's forces of production. Toward this end we must first overthrow the enemy. Second we must suppress its resistance. How could we do this without the revolutionary violence of the people?

Here the book turns to the "substance" of the proletarian dictatorship and the primary responsibilities of the working class and laboring people in general in the socialist revolution. But the discussion is incomplete as it leaves out the suppression of the enemy as well as the remolding of classes. Landlords, bureaucrats, counter-revolutionaries, and undesirable elements have to be remolded; the same holds true for the capitalist class, the upper stratum of the petit bourgeoisie, and the middle* peasants. Our experience shows that remolding is difficult. Those who do not undergo persistent repeated struggle can not be properly remolded. To eliminate thoroughly any remaining strength of the bourgeoisie and any influence they may have will take one or two decades at the least and may even require half a century. In the rural areas, where basic commune ownership has been put into effect, private ownership has been transformed into state

---

* Only in the 1969 text.

ownership. The entire country abounds with new cities and new major industry. Transportation and communications for the entire country have been modernized. Truly, the economic situation has been completely changed, and for the first time the peasants' worldview is bound to be turned around completely step by step. (Here in speaking of "primary responsibilities" the book uses Lenin's words differently from his original intention.)

To write or speak in an effort to suit the tastes of the enemy, the imperialists, is to defraud the masses and as a result to comfort the enemy while keeping one's own class in ignorance.

---

7. The Form of the Proletarian State

On page 334 the book says, "the proletarian state can take various forms." True enough, but there is not much difference essentially between the proletarian dictatorship in the people's democracies and the one established in Russia after the October Revolution. Also, the soviets of the Soviet Union and our own people's congresses were both representative assemblies, different in name only. In China the people's congresses included those participating as representatives of the bourgeoisie, representatives who had split off from the Nationalist Party, and representatives who were prominent democratic figures. All of them accepted the leadership of the Chinese Communist Party. One group among these tried to stir up trouble, but failed.[6] Such an inclusive form may appear different from the soviet, but it should be remembered that after the October Revolution the soviets included representatives of the Menshevik rightist Social Revolutionary Party, a Trotskyite faction, a Bukharin faction, a Zinoviev faction, and so forth. Nominally representatives of the workers and peasants, they were virtual representatives of the bourgeoisie. The period after the October Revolution was a time when the proletariat accepted a large number of personnel from the Kerensky government—all of whom were bourgeois elements. Our own central people's government was set up on the foundation of the North China People's Government. All members of the various departments were from the base areas, and the majority of the mainstay cadres were Communist Party members.

8. Transforming Capitalist Industry and Commerce

On page 335 there is an incorrect explanation of the process by which capitalist ownership changed into state ownership in China. The book only explains our policy toward national capital but not our policy toward bureaucratic capital (expropriation). In order to convert the property of the bureaucratic capitalist to public ownership we chose the method of expropriation.

In paragraph 2 of page 335 the experience of passing through the state capitalist form in order to transform capitalism is treated as a singular and special experience; its universal significance is denied. The countries of Western Europe and the United States have a very high level of capitalist development, and the controlling positions are held by a minority of monopoly capitalists. But there are a great number of small and middle capitalists as well. Thus it is said that American capital is concentrated but also widely distributed. After a successful revolution in these countries monopoly capital will undoubtedly have to be expropriated, but will the small and middle capitalists likewise be uniformly expropriated? It may well be the case that some form of state capitalism will have to be adopted to transform them.

Our northeast provinces may be thought of as a region with a high level of capitalist development. The same is true for Kiangsu (with centers in Shanghai and the southern part of the province). If state capitalism could work in these areas, tell me why the same policy could not work in other countries which resemble these provincial sectors?

The method the Japanese used when they held our northeast provinces was to eliminate the major local capitalists and turn their enterprises into Japanese state-managed, or in some cases monopoly capitalist enterprises. For the small and middle capitalists they established subsidiary companies as a means of imposing control.

Our transformation of national capital passed through three stages: private manufacture on state order, unified government purchase and sale of private output, joint state-private operation (of individual units and of whole complexes). Each phase was carried out in a methodical way. This prevented any damage to production, which actually developed as the transformation progressed. We have gained much new experience with state capitalism; for one example, the providing of capitalists with fixed interest after the joint state-private operation phase.[7]

9. Middle Peasants

After land reform, land was not worth money and the peasants were afraid to "show themselves." There were comrades who at one time considered this situation unsatisfactory, but what happened was that in the course of class struggles which disgraced landlords and rich peasants, the peasantry came to view poverty as dignified and wealth as shameful. This was a welcome sign, one which showed that the poor peasants had politically overturned the rich peasants and established their dominance in the villages.

On page 339 it says that the land taken from the rich peasants and given to the poor and middle peasants was land the government had expropriated and then parceled out. This looks at the matter as a grant by royal favor, forgetting that class struggles and mass mobilizations had been set in motion, a right deviationist point of view. Our approach was to rely on the poor peasants, to unite with the majority of middle peasants (lower middle peasants) and seize the land from the landlord class. While the party did play a leading role, it was against doing everything itself and thus substituting for the masses. Indeed, its concrete practice was to "pay call on the poor to learn of their grievances," to identify activist elements, to strike roots and pull things together, to consolidate nuclei, to promote the voicing of grievances, and to organize the class ranks—all for the purpose of unfolding the class struggle.

The text says "the middle peasants became the principal figures in the villages." This is an unsatisfactory assertion. To proclaim the middle peasants as the principals, commending them to the gods, never daring to offend them, is bound to make former poor peasants feel as if they had been put in the shade. Inevitably this opens the way for middle peasants of means to assume rural leadership.

The book makes no analysis of the middle peasant. We distinguish between upper and lower middle peasants and further between old and new within those categories, regarding the new as slightly preferable. Experience in campaign after campaign has shown that the poor peasant, the new lower middle peasant, and the old lower middle peasant have a comparatively good political attitude. They are the ones who embrace the people's communes. Among the upper middle peasants and the prosperous middle peasants there is a group that supports the communes as well as one that opposes them. According to materials from Hopei province the total number of production teams there comes to more than forty thousand, 50 percent of which embrace the communes without reservation, 35 percent of which basically accept them but with objections or doubts on particular questions, 15 percent of which oppose or have serious reservations about the communes. The opposition of this last group is due to the fact that the leadership of the teams fell to prosperous middle peasants or even undesirable elements. During this process of education in the struggle between the two roads, if the debate is to develop among these teams, their leadership will have to change. Clearly, then, the analysis of the middle peasant must be pursued. For the matter of whose hands hold rural leadership has tremendous bearing on the direction of developments there.

On page 340 the book says, "Essentially the middle peasant has a twofold character." This question also requires concrete analysis. The poor, lower middle, upper middle, and prosperous middle peasants in one sense are all workers, but in another they are private owners. As private owners their points of view are respectively dissimilar. Poor and lower middle peasants may be described as semiprivate owners whose point of view is comparatively easily altered. By contrast, the private owner's point of view held by the upper middle and the prosperous peasants has greater substance, and they have consistently resisted cooperativization.

10. The Worker-Peasant Alliance

The third and fourth paragraphs on page 340 are concerned with the importance of the worker-peasant alliance but fail to go into what must be done before the alliance can be developed and consolidated. The text, again, deals with the need of the peasants to press forward with the transformation of the small producers but fails to consider how to advance the process, what kinds of contradictions may be found at each stage of the transformation, and how they may be resolved. And, the text does not discuss the measures and tactics for the entire process.

Our worker-peasant alliance has already passed through two stages. The first was based on the land revolution, the second on the cooperative movement. If cooperativization had not been set in motion the peasantry inevitably would have been polarized, and the worker-peasant alliance could not have been consolidated. In consequence, the policy of "unified government purchase and sale of private output"[8] could not have been persevered in. The reason is that that policy could be maintained and made to work thoroughly only on the basis of cooperativization. At the present time our worker-peasant alliance has to take the next step and establish itself on the basis of mechanization. For to have simply the cooperative and commune movements without mechanization would once again mean that the alliance could not be consolidated. We still have to develop the cooperatives into people's communes. We still have to develop basic ownership by the commune team into basic ownership by the commune and that further into state ownership. When state ownership and mechanization are integrated we will be able to begin truly to consolidate the worker-peasant alliance, and the differences between workers and peasants will surely be eliminated step by step.

11. The Transformation of Intellectuals

Page 341 is devoted exclusively to the problem of fostering the development of intellectuals who are the workers' and peasants' own, as well as the problem of involving bourgeois intellectuals in socialist construction. However, the text fails to deal with the transformation of intellectuals. Not only the bourgeois intellectuals but even those of worker or peasant origin need to engage in transformation because they have come under the manifold influence of the bourgeoisie. Liu Shao-t'ang, of artistic and literary circles, who, after becoming an author, became a major opponent of socialism, exemplifies this. Intellectuals usually express their general outlook through their way of looking at knowledge. Is it privately owned or publicly owned? Some regard it as their own property, for sale when the price is right and not otherwise. Such are mere "experts" and not "reds"[9] who say the party is an "outsider" and "cannot lead the insiders." Those involved in the cinema claim that the party cannot lead the cinema. Those involved in musicals or ballet claim that the party cannot offer leadership there. Those in atomic science say the same. In sum, what they are all saying is that the party cannot lead anywhere. Remolding of the intellectuals is an extremely important question for the entire period of socialist revolution and construction. Of course it would be wrong to minimize this question or to adopt a concessive attitude toward things bourgeois.

Again on page 341 it says that the fundamental contradiction in the transition economy is the one between capitalism and socialism. Correct. But this passage speaks only of setting struggles in motion to see who will emerge the victor in all realms of economic life. None of this is complete. We would put it as follows: a thoroughgoing socialist revolution must advance along the three fronts of politics, economics, and ideology.

The text says that we absorb bourgeois elements so that they may participate in the management of enterprises and the state. This is repeated on page 357.* But we insist on the responsibility for remolding the bourgeois elements. We help them change their lifestyle, their general outlook, and also their viewpoint on particular issues. The text, however, makes no mention of remolding.

12. The Relationship Between Industrialization and Agricultural Collectivization

The book sees socialist industrialization as the precondition for agricultural collectivization. This view in no way corresponds to the situation in the Soviet Union itself, where collectivization was basically realized between 1930 and 1932. Though they had then more tractors than we do now, still and all the amount of arable land under mechanized cultivation was under 20.3 percent. Collectivization is not altogether determined by mechanization, and so industrialization is not the precondition for it.

Agricultural collectivization in the socialist countries of Eastern Europe was completed very slowly, mainly because after land reform, they did not strike while the iron was hot but delayed for a time. In some of our own old base areas, too, a section of the peasantry was satisfied with the reform and unwilling to proceed further. This situation did not depend at all on whether or not there was industrialization.

13. War and Revolution

On pages 352–54 it is argued that the various people's democracies of Eastern Europe "were able to build socialism

---

*Page 341, according to the 1967 text.

even though there was neither civil war nor armed intervention from abroad." It is also argued that "socialist transformation in these countries was realized without the ordeal of civil war." It would have been better to say that what happened in these countries is that a civil war was waged in the form of international war, that civil and international war were waged together. The reactionaries of these countries were ploughed under by the Soviet Red Army. To say that there was no civil war in these countries would be mere formalism that disregards substance.

The text says that in the countries of Eastern Europe after the revolution "parliaments became the organs for broadly representing the people's interests." In fact, these parliaments were completely different from the bourgeois parliaments of old, bearing resemblance in name only. The Political Consultative Conference we had during the early phase of Liberation was no different in name from the Political Consultative Conference of the Nationalist period. During our negotiations with the Nationalists we were indifferent to the conference but Chiang Kai-shek was very interested in it. After Liberation we took over their singboard and called into session a nationwide Chinese People's Political Consultative Conference, which served as a provisional people's congress.[10]

The text says that China "in the process of revolutionary struggle organized a people's democratic united front." (p. 357) Why only "revolutionary struggle" and not "revolutionary war?" From 1927 down to the nationwide victory we waged twenty-two years of long-term uninterrupted war. And even before that, starting with the bourgeois revolution of 1911, there was another fifteen years' warfare. The chaotic wars of the warlords under the direction of imperialists should also be counted. Thus, from 1911 down to the War to Resist America and Aid Korea, it may be said that continual wars were waged in China for forty years—revolutionary warfare and counter-revolutionary warfare. And, since its founding, our party has joined or led wars for thirty years.

A great revolution must go through a civil war. This is a

rule. And to see the ills of war but not its benefits is a one-sided view. It is of no use to the people's revolution to speak onesidedly of the destructiveness of war.

14. Is Revolution Harder in Backward Countries?

In the various nations of the West there is a great obstacle to carrying through any revolution and construction movement; i.e., the poisons of the bourgeoisie are so powerful that they have penetrated each and every corner. While our bourgeoisie has had, after all, only three generations, those of England and France have had a 250–300 year history of development, and their ideology and *modus operandi* have influenced all aspects and strata of their societies. Thus the English working class follows the Labour Party, not the Communist Party.

Lenin says, "The transition from capitalism to socialism will be more difficult for a country the more backward it is." This would seem incorrect today. Actually, the transition is less difficult the more backward an economy is, for the poorer they are the more the people want revolution. In the capitalist countries of the West the number of people employed is comparatively high, and so is the wage level. Workers there have been deeply influenced by the bourgeoisie, and it would not appear to be all that easy to carry through a socialist transformation. And since the degree of mechanization is high, the major problem after a successful revolution would not be advancing mechanization but transforming the people. Countries of the East, such as China and Russia, had been backward and poor, but now not only have their social systems moved well ahead of those of the West, but even the rate of development of their productive forces far outstrips that of the West. Again, as in the history of the development of the capitalist countries, the backward overtake the advanced as America overtook England, and as Germany later overtook England early in the twentieth century.

15. Is Large-Scale Industry the Foundation of Socialist Transformation?

On page 364* the text says, "Countries that have taken the road of socialist construction face the task of eliminating as quickly as possible the aftereffects of capitalist rule in order to accelerate the development of large industry (the basis for the socialist transformation of the economy)." It is not enough to assert that the development of large industry is the foundation for the socialist transformation of the economy. All revolutionary history shows that the full development of new productive forces is not the prerequisite for the transformation of backward production relations. Our revolution began with Marxist-Leninist propaganda, which served to create new public opinion in favor of the revolution. Moreover, it was possible to destroy the old production relations only after we had overthrown a backward superstructure in the course of revolution. After the old production relations had been destroyed new ones were created, and these cleared the way for the development of new social productive forces. With that behind us we were able to set in motion the technological revolution to develop social productive forces on a large scale. At the same time, we still had to continue transforming the production relations and ideology.

This textbook addresses itself only to material preconditions and seldom engages the question of the superstructure, i.e., the class nature of the state, philosophy, and science. In economics the main object of study is the production relations. All the same, political economy and the materialist historical outlook are close cousins. It is difficult to deal clearly with problems of the economic base and the production relations if the question of the superstructure is neglected.

---

* Page 349, according to the 1967 text.

16. *Lenin's Discussion of the Unique Features of Taking the Socialist Road*

On page 375 a passage from Lenin is cited. It is well expressed and quite helpful for defending our work methods. "The level of consciousness of the residents, together with the efforts they have made to realize this or that plan, are bound to be reflected in the unique features of the road they take toward socialism." Our own "politics in command" is precisely for raising the consciousness in our neighborhoods. Our own Great Leap Forward is precisely an "effort to realize this or that plan."

17. *The Rate of Industrialization Is a Critical Problem*

The text says, "As far as the Soviet Union is concerned, the rate of industrialization is a critical problem." At present this is a critical problem for China, too. As a matter of fact, the problem becomes more acute the more backward industry is. This is true not only from country to country but also from one area to another in the same country. For example, our northeastern provinces and Shanghai have a comparatively strong base, and so state investment increased somewhat less rapidly there. In other areas, where the original industrial base was slight, and development was urgently needed, state investment increased quite rapidly. In the ten years that Shanghai has been liberated 2.2 billion Chinese dollars[11] have been invested, over 500 million by capitalists. Shanghai used to have over half a million workers, now the city has over 1 million, if we do not count the hundreds of thousands transferred out. This is only double the earlier worker population. When we compare this with certain new cities where the work force has increased enormously we can see plainly that in areas with a deficient industrial base the problem of rate is all the more critical. Here the text only says that political circumstances demand the high rate and does not explain whether or not the socialist system itself can attain the high rate. This is onesided. If there is only the need and not the capability, tell me, how is the high rate to be achieved? [12]

18. Achieve a High Rate of Industrialization by Concurrent Promotion of Small, Medium, and Large Enterprise

On page 381 the text touches on our broad development of small- and medium-scale enterprise but fails to reflect accurately our philosophy of concurrent promotion of native and foreign, small, medium, and large enterprise. The text says we "determined upon extensive development of small- and medium-scale enterprises because of the utter backwardness of our technological economy, the size of our populations and very serious employment problems." But the problem by no means lies in technological age, population size, or the need to increase employment. Under the guidance of the larger enterprises we are developing the small and the medium; under the guidance of the foreign we are adopting native methods wherever we can—mainly for the sake of achieving the high rate of industrialization.

19. Is Long-Term Coexistence Between Two Types of Socialist Ownership Possible?

On page 386 it says, "A socialist state and socialist construction can not be established on two different bases for any length of time. That is to say, they can not be established on the base of socialist industry, the largest and most unified base, *and* on the base of the peasant petty commodity economy, which is scattered and backward." This point is well taken, of course, and we therefore extend the logic to reach the following conclusion: The socialist state and socialist construction cannot be established for any great length of time on the basis of ownership by the whole people *and* ownership by the collective as two different bases of ownership.

In the Soviet Union the period of coexistence between the

two types of ownership has lasted too long. The contradictions between ownership of the whole people and collective ownership are in reality contradictions between workers and peasants. The text fails to recognize such contradictions.

In the same way prolonged coexistence of ownership by the whole people with ownership by the collectives is bound to become less and less adaptable to the development of the productive forces and will fail to satisfy the ever increasing needs of peasant consumption and agricultural production or of industry for raw materials. To satisfy such needs we must resolve the contradiction between these two forms of ownership, transform ownership by the collectives into ownership by the whole people, and make a unified plan for production and distribution in industry and agriculture on the basis of ownership by the whole people for an indivisible nation.

The contradictions between the productive forces and the production relations unfold without interruption. Relations that once were adapted to the productive forces will no longer be so after a period of time. In China, after we finished organizing the advanced cooperatives, the question of having both large and small units came up in every special district and in every county.

In socialist society the formal categories of distribution according to labor, commodity production, the law of value, and so forth are presently adapted to the demands of the productive forces. But as this development proceeds, the day is sure to come when these formal categories will no longer be adapted. At that time these categories will be destroyed by the development of the productive forces; their life will be over. Are we to believe that in a socialist society there are economic categories that are eternal and unchanging? Are we to believe that such categories as distribution according to labor and collective ownership are eternal—unlike all other categories, which are historical [hence relative]?

20. *The Socialist Transformation of Agriculture Cannot Depend Only on Mechanization*

Page 392 states, "The machine and tractor stations are important tools for carrying through the socialist transformation in agriculture." Again and again the text emphasizes how important machinery is for the transformation. But if the consciousness of the peasantry is not raised, if ideology is not transformed, and you are depending on nothing but machinery—what good will it be? The question of the struggle between the two roads, socialism and capitalism, the transformation and re-education of people—these are the major questions for China.

The text on page 395 says that in carrying through the tasks of the early stages of general collectivization the question of the struggle against hostile rich peasants comes up. This of course is correct. But in the account the text gives of rural conditions *after* the formation of cooperatives the question of a prosperous stratum is dropped, nor is there any mention of such contradictions as those between the state, the collectives, and individuals, between accumulation and consumption,[13] and so forth.

Page 402 says, "Under conditions of high tide in the agricultural cooperative movement the broad masses of the middle peasantry will not waver again." This is too general. There is a section of rich middle peasants that is now wavering and will do so in the future.

21. *So-Called Full Consolidation*

". . . fully consolidated the collective farm system," it says on page 407. "Full consolidation"—a phrase to make one uneasy. The consolidation of anything is relative. How can it be "full"? What if no one died since the beginning of mankind, and everyone got "fully consolidated"? What kind of a world would that be! In the universe, on our globe, all things come into being, develop, and pass away ceaselessly. None of them is ever "fully consolidated." Take the life of a silkworm. Not only must it pass away in the end, it must pass through four stages of development during its lifetime: egg, silkworm, pupa, moth. It must move on from one stage to the next and can never fully consolidate itself in any one stage. In the end, the moth dies, and its old essence becomes a new essence (as it leaves behind many eggs). This is a qualitative leap. Of course, from egg to worm, from worm to pupa, from pupa to moth clearly are more than quantitative changes. There is qualitative transformation too, but it is *partial* qualitative transformation. A person, too, in the process of moving through life toward death, experiences different stages: childhood, adolescence, youth, adulthood and old age. From life to death is a quantitative process for people, but at the same time they are pushing forward the process of partial qualitative change. It would be absurd to think that from youth to old age is but a quantitative increase without qualitative change. Inside the human organism cells are ceaselessly dividing, old ones dying and vanishing, new ones emerging and growing. At death there is a complete qualitative change, one that has come about through the preceding quantitative changes as well as the partial qualitative changes that occur during the quantitative changes. Quantitative change and qualitative change are a unity of opposites. Within the quantitative changes there are partial qualitative changes. One cannot say that there are no qualitative changes within quantitative changes. And within qualitative changes there are quantitative changes. One cannot say that there are no quantitative changes within qualitative changes.

In any lengthy process of change, before entering the final qualitative change, the subject must pass through uninterrupted quantitative changes and a good many partial qualitative changes. But the final qualitative change cannot come about unless there are partial qualitative changes and considerable quantitative change. For example, a factory of a given plant and size changes qualitatively as the machinery and other installations are renovated a section at a time. The interior changes even though the exterior and the size do not. A company of soldiers is no different. After it has fought a battle and lost dozens of men, a hundred-soldier company will have to replace its casualties. Fighting and replenishing continuously—this is how the company goes through uninterrupted partial qualitative change. As a result the company continues to develop and harden itself.

The crushing of Chiang Kai-shek was a qualitative change which came about through quantitative change. For example, there had to be a three-and-a-half-year period during which his army and political power were destroyed a section at a time. And, within this quantitative change qualitative change is to be found. The War of Liberation went through several different stages, and each new stage differed qualitatively from the preceding stages. The transformation from individual to collective economy was a process of qualitative transformation. In our country this process consisted of mutual aid teams, early-stage cooperatives, advanced cooperatives, and people's communes.[14] Such different stages of partial qualitative change brought a collective economy out of an individual economy.

The present socialist economy in our country is organized through two different forms of public ownership, ownership by the whole people and collective ownership. This socialist economy has had its own birth and development. Who would believe that this process of change has come to an end, and that we will say, "These two forms of ownership will continue to be fully consolidated for all time?" Who would believe that such formulas of a socialist society as "distribution according to labor," "commodity production," and "the law of value" are going to live forever? Who would believe that there is only birth and development but no dying away and transformation and that these formulas unlike all others are ahistorical?

Socialism must make the transition to communism. At that time there will be things of the socialist stage that will have to die out. And, too, in the period of communism there will still be uninterrupted development. It is quite possible that communism will have to pass through a number of different stages. How can we say that once communism has been reached nothing will change, that everything will continue "fully consolidated," that there will be quantitative change only, and no partial qualitative change going on all the time.

The way things develop, one stage leads on to another, advancing without interruption. But each and every stage has a "boundary." Every day we read from, say, four o'clock and end at seven or eight. That is the boundary. As far as socialist ideological remolding goes, it is a long-term task. But each ideological campaign reaches its conclusion, that is to say, has a boundary. On the ideological front, when we will have come through uninterrupted quantitative changes and partial qualitative changes, the day will arrive when we will be completely free of the influence of capitalist ideology. At that time the qualitative changes of ideological remolding will have ended, but only to be followed by the quantitative changes of a *new* quality.

The construction of socialism also has its boundary. We have to keep tabs: for example, what is to be the ratio of industrial goods to total production, how much steel is to be produced, how high can the people's living standard be raised, etc.? But to say that socialist construction has a boundary hardly means that we do not want to take the next step, to make the transition to communism. It is possible to divide the transition from capitalism to communism into two stages: one from capitalism to socialism, which could be called underdeveloped socialism; and one from socialism to communism, that is, from comparatively underdeveloped socialism to comparatively developed socialism, namely, communism. This latter stage may take even longer than the first. But once it has been passed through, material production and spiritual prosperity will be most ample. People's communist consciousness will be greatly raised, and they will be ready to enter the highest stage of communism.

On page 409 it says that after the forms of socialist production have been firmly established, production will steadily and rapidly expand. The rate of productivity will climb steadily. The text uses the term *steadily* or *without interruption* a good many times, but only to speak of quantitative transformation. There is little mention of partial qualitative change.

22. War and Peace

On page 408 it says that in capitalist societies "a crisis of surplus production will inevitably be created, causing unemployment to increase." This is the gestation of war. It is difficult to believe that the basic principles of Marxist economics are suddenly without effect, that in a world where capitalist institutions still exist war can be fully eliminated.

Can it be said that the possibility of eliminating war for good has now arisen? Can it be said that the possibility of plying all the world's wealth and resources to the service of mankind has arisen? This view is not Marxism, it has no class analysis, and it has not distinguished clearly between conditions under bourgeois and proletarian rule. If you do not eliminate classes, how can you eliminate war?

We will not be the ones to determine whether a world war will be waged or not. Even if a nonbelligerency agreement is signed, the possibility of war will still exist. When imperialism wants to fight no agreement is going to be taken into account. And, if it comes, whether atomic or hydrogen weapons will be used is yet another question. Even though chemical weapons exist, they have not been used in time of war; conventional weapons were used after all. Even if there is no war between the two camps, there is no guarantee war will not be waged within the capitalist world. Imperialism may make war on imperialism. The bourgeoisie of one imperialist country may make war on its proletariat. Imperialism is even now waging war against colony and semicolony. War is one form of class conflict. But classes will not be eliminated except through war. And war cannot be eliminated for good except through the elimination of classes. If revolutionary war is not carried on, classes cannot be eliminated. We do not believe that the weapons of war can be eliminated without destroying classes. It is not possible. In the history of class societies any class or state is concerned with its "position of strength." Gaining such positions has been history's inevitable tendency. Armed force is the concrete manifestation of the real strength of a class. And as long as there is class antagonism there will be armed forces. Naturally, we are not wishing for war. We wish for peace. We favor making the utmost effort to stop nuclear war and to strive for a mutual nonaggression pact between the two camps. To strive to gain even ten or twenty years' peace was what we advocated long ago. If we can realize this wish, it would be most beneficial for the entire socialist camp and for China's socialist construction as well.

On page 409 it says that at this time the Soviet Union is no longer encircled by capitalism. This manner of speaking runs the risk of lulling people to sleep. Of course the present situation has changed greatly from when there was only one socialist country. West of the Soviet Union there are now the various socialist countries of Eastern Europe. East of the Soviet Union are the socialist countries of China, Korea, Mongolia, and Vietnam. But the guided missiles have no eyes and can strike targets thousands or tens of thousands of kilometers away. All around the socialist camp American military bases are deployed, pointed toward the Soviet Union and the other socialist countries. Can it be said that the Soviet Union is no longer inside the ring of missiles?

23. Is Unanimity the Motive Force of Social Development?

On page 413 and 417 it says that socialism makes for the "solidarity of unanimity" and is "hard as a rock." It says that unanimity is the "motive force of social development."

This recognizes only the unanimity of solidarity but not the contradictions within a socialist society, nor that contradiction is the motive force of social development. Once it is put this way, the law of the universality of contradiction is denied, the laws of dialectics are suspended. Without contradictions there is no movement, and society always develops through movement. In the era of socialism, contradictions remain the motive force of social development. Precisely because there is no unanimity there is the responsibility for unity, the necessity to fight for it. If there were 100 percent unanimity always, then what explains the necessity for persevering in working for unity?

24. Rights of Labor Under Socialism

On page 414 we find a discussion of the rights labor enjoys but no discussion of labor's right to run the state, the various enterprises, education, and culture. Actually, this is labor's greatest right under socialism, the most fundamental right, without which there is no right to work, to an education, to vacation, etc.

The paramount issue for socialist democracy is: Does labor have the right to subdue the various antagonistic forces and their influences? For example, who controls things like the newspapers, journals, broadcast stations, the cinema? Who criticizes? These are a part of the question of rights. If these things are in the hands of right opportunists (who are a minority) then the vast nationwide majority that urgently needs a great leap forward will find itself deprived of these rights. If the cinema is in the hands of people like Chung Tien-p'ei,[15] how are the people supposed to realize their own rights in that sector? There is a variety of factions among the people. Who is in control of the organs and enterprises bears tremendously on the issue of guaranteeing the people's rights. If Marxist-Leninists are in control, the rights of the vast majority will be guaranteed. If rightists or right opportunists are in control, these organs and enterprises may change qualitatively, and the people's rights with respect to them cannot be guaranteed. In sum, the people must have the right to manage the superstructure. We must not take the rights of the people to mean that the state is to be managed by only a section of the people, that the people can enjoy labor rights, education rights, social insurance, etc., only under the management of certain people.

25. *Is the Transition to Communism a Revolution?*

On page 417 it says, "Under socialism there will be no class or social group whose interests conflict with communism and therefore the transition to communism will come about without social revolution."

The transition to communism certainly is not a matter of one class overthrowing another. But that does not mean there will be no social revolution, because the superseding of one kind of production relations by another is a qualitative leap, i.e., a revolution. The two transformations—of individual economy to collective, and collective economy to public—in China are both revolutions in the production relations. So to go from socialism's "distribution according to labor" to communism's "distribution according to need" has to be called a revolution in the production relations. Of course, "distribution according to need" has to be brought about gradually. Perhaps when the principal material goods can be adequately supplied we can begin to carry out such distribution with those goods, extending the practice to other goods on the basis of further development of the productive forces.

Consider the development of our people's communes. When we changed from basic ownership by the team to basic ownership by the commune, was a section of the people likely to raise objections or not? This is a question well worth our study. A determinative condition for realizing this changeover was that the commune-owned economy's income was more than half of the whole commune's total income. To realize the basic commune-ownership system is generally of benefit to the members of the commune. Thus we estimate that there should be no objection on the part of the vast majority. But at the time of changeover the original team cadres could no longer be relatively reduced under the circumstances. Would *they* object to the changeover?

Although classes may be eliminated in a socialist society, in the course of its development there are bound to be certain problems with "vested interest groups" which have grown content with existing institutions and unwilling to change them. For example, if the rule of distribution according to labor is in effect they benefit from higher pay for more work, and when it came time to change over to "distribution according to need" they could very well be uncomfortable with the new situation. Building any new system always necessitates some destruction of old ones. Creation never comes without destruction. If destruction is necessary it is bound to arouse some opposition. The human animal is queer indeed. No sooner do people gain some superiority than they assume airs . . . it would be dangerous to ignore this.

26. The Claim That "for China There Is No Necessity to Adopt Acute Forms of Class Struggle"

There is an error on page 419. After the October Revolution Russia's bourgeoisie saw that the country's economy had suffered severe damage, and so they decided that the proletariat could not change the situation and lacked the strength to maintain its political power. They judged that they only had to make the move and proletarian political power could be overthrown. At this point they carried out armed resistance, thus compelling the Russian proletariat to take drastic steps to expropriate their property. At that time neither class had much experience.

To say that China's class struggle is not acute is unrealistic. It was fierce enough! We fought for twenty-two years straight. By waging war we overthrew the rule of the bourgeoisie's Nationalist Party, and expropriated bureaucratic capital, which amounted to 80 percent of our entire capitalist economy. Only thus was it possible for us to use peaceful methods to remold the remaining 20 percent of national capital. In the remolding process we still had to go through such fierce struggles as the "three-antis" and the "five-antis" campaigns.[16]

Page 420 incorrectly describes the remolding of bourgeois

industrial and commercial enterprises. After Liberation the national bourgeoisie was forced to take the road of socialist remolding. We brought down Chiang Kai-shek, expropriated bureaucratic capital, concluded the land reform, carried out the "three-antis" and "five-antis" campaigns, and made the cooperatives a working reality. We controlled the markets from the beginning. This series of transformations forced the national bourgeoisie to accept remolding step by step. From yet another point of view, the Common Program stipulated that various kinds of economic interests were to be given scope. This enabled the capitalists to try for what profits they could. In addition, the constitution gave them the right to a ballot and a living. These things helped the bourgeoisie to realize that by accepting remolding they could hold onto a social position and also play a certain role in the culture and in the economy.

In joint state-private enterprises the capitalists have no real managerial rights over the enterprise. Production is certainly not jointly managed by the capitalists and representatives of the public. Nor can it be said that "Capital's exploitation of labor has been limited." It has been virtually curtailed. The text seems to have missed the idea that the jointly operated enterprises we are speaking of were 75 percent socialist. Of course at present they are 90 percent socialist or more.

The remolding of capitalist industry and commerce has been basically concluded. But if the capitalists had the chance they would attack us without restraint. In 1957 we pushed back the onslaught of the right.[17] In 1959, through their representatives in the party, they again set in motion an attack against us.[18] Our policy toward the national capitalists is to take them along with us and then to encompass them.

The text uses Lenin's statement that state capitalism "continues the class struggle in another form." This is correct. (p. 421)

27. *The Time Period for Building Socialism*

On page 423 it says that we "concluded" the socialist revolution on the political and ideological fronts in 1957.[19] We would rather say that we won a decisive victory.

On the same page it says that we want to turn China into a strong socialist country within ten to fifteen years. Now this is something we agree on! This means that after the second five-year plan we will have to go through another two five-year plans until 1972 (or 1969 if we strive to beat the schedule by two or three years). In addition to modernizing industry and agriculture, science and culture, we have to modernize national defense. In a country such as ours bringing the building of socialism to its conclusion is a tremendously difficult task. In socialist construction we must not speak of "early."

28. *Further Discussion of the Relationship Between Industrialization and Socialist Transformation*

On page 423 it says that reform of the system of ownership long before the realization of industrialization was a circumstance created by special conditions in China. This is an error. Eastern Europe, like China, "benefited from the existence of the mighty socialist camp and the help of an industrialized country as developed as the Soviet Union." The question is, what was the reason Eastern European countries could not complete the socialist transformation in the ownership system (including agriculture) before industrialization became a reality?* Turning to the relationship between in-

---

* Cf. Chapter 28, paragraph 1, of the 1967 edition:

Page 423 says, "Given the special conditions in China, before socialist industrialization became a reality, it was thanks to the existence of the mighty socialist camp and the help of a powerful, highly developed industrial nation like the Soviet Union that the reform of the ownership system (including agriculture) achieved victory." This is an error. The countries of Eastern

dustrialization and socialist transformation, the truth is that in the Soviet Union itself the problem of ownership was settled before industrialization became a reality.

Similarly, from the standpoint of world history, the bourgeois revolutions and the establishment of the bourgeois nations came before, not after, the Industrial Revolution. The bourgeoisie first changed the superstructure and took possession of the machinery of state before carrying on propaganda to gather real strength. Only then did they push forward great changes in the production relations. When the production relations had been taken care of and they were on the right track they then opened the way for the development of the productive forces. To be sure, the revolution in the production relations is brought on by a certain degree of development of the productive forces, but the major development of the productive forces always comes after changes in the production relations. Consider the history of the development of capitalism. First came simple coordination, which subsequently developed into workshop handicrafts. At this time capitalist production relations were already taking shape, but the workshops produced without machines. This type of capitalist production relations gave rise to the need for technological advance, creating the conditions for the use of machinery. In England the Industrial Revolution (late eighteenth-early nineteenth centuries) was carried through only after the bourgeois revolution, that is, after the seventeenth century. All in their respective ways, Germany, France, America, and Japan underwent change in superstructure and production relations before the vast development of capitalist industry.

It is a general rule that you cannot solve the problem of ownership and go on to expand development of the productive forces until you have first prepared public opinion for the seizure of political power. Although between the bourgeois

Europe no less than China "had the existence of the powerful socialist camp and the help of as highly developed an industrial nation as the Soviet Union." Why could they not complete socialist transformation in the ownership system (including agriculture) before industrialization became a reality?

revolution and the proletarian revolution there are certain differences (before the proletarian revolution socialist production relations did not exist, while capitalist production relations were already beginning to grow in feudal society), basically they are alike.

PART II: CHAPTERS 24–29

29. Contradictions Between Socialist Production Relations and Productive Forces

Page 433 discusses only the "mutual function" of the production relations and the productive forces under socialism but not the contradictions between them. The production relations include ownership of the means of production, the relations among people in the course of production, and the distribution system. The revolution in the system of ownership is the base, so to speak. For example, after the entire national economy has become indivisibly owned by the whole people through the transition from collective to people's ownership, although people's ownership will certainly be in effect for a relatively long time, for all enterprises so owned important problems will remain. Should a central-local division of authority be in effect? Which enterprises should be managed by whom? In 1958 in some basic construction units a system of fixed responsibility for capital investment was put into effect. The result was a tremendous release of enthusiasm in these units. When the center cannot depend on its own initiative it must release the enthusiasm of the enterprise or the locality. If such enthusiasm is frustrated it hurts production.

We see then that contradictions to be resolved remain in the production relations under people's ownership. As far as relations among people in the course of labor and the distribution relations go, it is all the more necessary to improve them unremittingly. For these areas it is rather difficult to say what the base is. Much remains to be written about human relations in the course of labor, e.g., concerning the leadership's adopting egalitarian attitudes, the changing of

certain regulations and established practices, "the two participations" [worker participation in management and management participation in productive labor], "the three combinations" [combining efforts of cadres, workers, and techni-
cians], etc. Public ownership of primitive communes lasted
a long time, but during that time people's relations to each
other underwent a good many changes, all the same, in the
course of labor.

---

30. The Transition from Collective to People's Ownership Is Inevitable

---

On page 435 the text says only that the existence of two
forms of public ownership is objectively inevitable, but not
that the transition from collective to people's ownership is
also objectively inevitable. This is an inescapable objective
process, one presently in evidence in certain areas of our
country. According to data from Cheng An county in Hopei
province, communes growing industrial crops are thriving,
accumulation levels have been raised to 45 percent,[20] and the
peasants' living standard is high. Should this situation continue to develop, if we do not let collective ownership become
people's ownership and resolve the contradiction, peasant living standards will surpass those of the workers to the detri-
ment of both industrial and agricultural development.

On page 438 it says that "state-managed enterprises are
not fundamentally different from cooperatives. . . . there
exist two forms of public ownership. . . . sacred and inviolable." There *is* no difference between collective and people's ownership with reference to capitalism, but the difference becomes fundamental within the socialist economy.
The text speaks of the two forms of ownership as "sacred and
inviolable." This is allowable when speaking of hostile forces,
but when speaking of the process of development of public
ownership it becomes wrong. Nothing can be regarded as
unchanging. Ownership by the whole people itself also has a
process of change.

After a good many years, after ownership by the people's

communes has changed into ownership by the whole people, the whole nation will become an indivisible system of ownership by the whole people. This will greatly spur the development of the productive forces. For a period of time this will remain a *socialist* system of ownership by the whole people, and only after another period will it be a *communist* system of ownership by the whole people. Thus, people's ownership itself will have to progress from distribution according to labor to distribution according to need.

31. Individual Property

On page 439 it says, "Another part is consumer goods. . . . which make up the personal property of the workers." This manner of expression tends to make people think that goods classified as "consumer" are to be distributed to the workers as their individual property. This is incorrect. One part of consumer goods is individual property, another is public property, e.g., cultural and educational facilities, hospitals, athletic facilities, parks, etc. Moreover, this part is increasing. Of course they are for each worker to enjoy, but they are not individual property.

On page 440 we find lumped together work income and savings, housing, household goods, goods for individual consumption, and other ordinary equipment. This is unsatisfactory because savings, housing, etc. are all derived from working people's incomes.

In too many places this book speaks only of individual consumption and not of social consumption, such as public welfare, culture, health, etc. This is onesided. Housing in our rural areas is far from what it should be. We must improve rural dwelling conditions in an orderly fashion.* Residential construction, particularly in cities, should in the main use collective social forces, not individual ones. If a socialist society does not undertake collective efforts what kind of socialism is there in the end? Some say that socialism is more con-

---

*Only in the 1969 text.

cerned with material incentives than capitalism. Such talk is simply outrageous.

Here the text says that the wealth produced by collective farms includes individual property as well as subsidiary occupations. If we fail to propose transforming these subsidiary occupations into public ownership, the peasants will be peasants forever. A given social system must be consolidated in a given period of time. But consolidation must have a limit. If it goes on and on, the ideology reflecting the system is bound to become rigidified, causing the people to be unable to adjust their thinking to new developments.

On the same page there is mention of integrating individual and collective interests. It says, "Integration is realized by the following method: a member of society is compensated according to the quantity and quality of his labor so as to satisfy the principle of individual material interest." Here, without discussion of the necessary reservations, the text places individual interest first. This is onesided treatment of the principle of individual material interest.

According to page 441, "Public and individual interests are not at odds and can be gradually resolved." This is spoken in vain and solves nothing. In a country like ours, if the contradictions among the people are not put to rights every few years, they will never get resolved.

32. Contradiction Is the Motive Force of Development in a Socialist Society

Page 443, paragraph 5, admits that in a socialist society contradictions between the productive forces and the production relations exist and speaks of overcoming such contradictions. But by no means does the text recognize that contradictions are the motive force.

The succeeding paragraph is acceptable; however, under socialism it is not only certain aspects of human relations and certain forms of leading the economy, but also problems of the ownership system itself (e.g., the two types of ownership) that may hinder the development of the productive forces.

Most dubious is the viewpoint in the next paragraph. It says, "The contradictions under socialism are not irreconcilable." This does not agree with the laws of dialectics, which hold that all contradictions are irreconcilable. Where has there ever been a reconcilable contradiction? Some are antagonistic, some are nonantagonistic, but it must not be thought that there are irreconcilable and reconcilable contradictions.

Under socialism* there may be no war but there is still struggle, struggle among sections of the people; there may be no revolution of one class overthrowing another, but there is still revolution. The transition from socialism to communism is revolutionary. The transition from one stage of communism to another is also. Then there is technological revolution and cultural revolution. Communism will surely have to pass through many stages and many revolutions.

Here the text speaks of relying on the "positive action" of the masses to overcome contradictions at the proper time. "Positive action" should include complicated struggles.

"Under socialism there is no class energetically plotting to preserve outmoded economic relations." Correct, but in a socialist society there are still conservative strata and something like "vested interest groups." There still remain differences between mental and manual labor, city and countryside, worker and peasant. Although these are not antagonistic contradictions they cannot be resolved without struggle.

The children of our cadres are a cause of discouragement. They lack experience of life and of society, yet their airs are considerable and they have a great sense of superiority. They have to be educated not to rely on their parents or martyrs of the past but entirely on themselves.

In a socialist society there are always advanced and backward persons, those who are steadfastly loyal to the collective effort, diligent and sincere, fresh of spirit and lively, and

---

* The transcriber of the 1967 text comments that Mao may have meant "under communism."

those who are acting for fame and fortune, for the personal end, for the self, or who are apathetic and dejected. In the course of socialist development each and every period is bound to have a group that is more than willing to preserve backward production relations and social institutions. On many many questions the prosperous middle peasants have their own point of view. They cannot adapt to new developments, and some of them resist such developments, as proved by the debate over the Eight-Word Constitution[21] with the prosperous peasants of the Kuangtung rural areas.

Page 453, the last paragraph, says, "Criticism and self-criticism are powerful motive forces for the development of socialist society." This is not the point. Contradictions are the motive forces, criticism and self-criticism are the methods for resolving contradictions.

33. The Dialectical Process of Knowledge

Page 446, paragraph 2, says that as ownership becomes public "people become the masters of the economic relations of their own society," and are "able to take hold of and apply these laws fully and consciously." It should be observed that this requires going through a process. The understanding of laws always begins with the understanding of a minority before it becomes the knowledge of the majority. It is necessary to go through a process of practice and study to go from ignorance to knowledge. At the beginning no one has knowledge. Foreknowledge has never existed. People must go through practice to gain results, meet with failure as problems arise; only through such a process can knowledge gradually advance. If you want to know the objective laws of the development of things and events you must go through the process of practice, adopt a Marxist-Leninist attitude, compare successes and failures, continually practicing and studying, going through multiple successes and failures; moreover, meticulous research must be performed. There is no other way to make one's own knowledge gradually conform to the laws. For those who see only victory but not defeat it will not be possible to know these laws.

It is not easy "to possess and apply these laws fully and consciously." On page 446 the text quotes Engels. "Only at this time does the fully conscious self begin to create history. For the first time to a great extent and to an ever greater extent people can create the effects they aspire after." "Begin to" and "to an ever greater extent" are relatively accurate.

The text does not recognize the contradictions between appearances and essences. Essences always lie behind appearances and cannot be disclosed except through appearances. The text does not express the idea that for a person to know the laws it is necessary to go through a process. The vanguard is no exception.

34. Unions and the Single Leadership System

On page 452 when speaking of the mission of trade unions, the text does not say that the primary task of the unions is to develop production; it does not discuss ways to strengthen political education; it merely overemphasizes welfare.

Throughout, the text speaks of "managing production according to the principle of the single-leader system." All enterprises in capitalist countries put this principle into effect. There should be a basic distinction between the principles governing management of socialist and capitalist enterprises. We in China have been able to distinguish our methods strictly from capitalist management by putting into effect factory leader responsibility under the guidance of the party.

35. Starting from Fundamental Principles and Rules Is Not the Marxist Method

From the second chapter on a great many rules are set up. The analysis of capitalist economy in *Das Kapital* commences with appearances, searches out essences, and only then uses the essence to explain the appearance, making through this method effective summaries and outlines. But the text does not pursue an analysis. Its composition lacks order. It always proceeds from rules, principles, laws, definitions, a methodology Marxism-Leninism has always opposed.

The *effects* of principles and laws must be subjected to analysis and thorough study; only then can principles and laws be derived. Human knowledge always encounters appearances first. Proceeding from there, one searches out principles and laws. The text does the opposite. Its methodology is deductive, not analytical. According to formal logic, "People all will die. Mr. Chang is a person. Therefore Mr. Chang will die." This is a conclusion derived from the premise that all human beings die. This is the deductive method. For every question the text first gives definitions, which it then takes as a major premise and reasons from there, failing to understand that the major premise should be the result of researching a question. Not until one has gone through the concrete research can principles and laws be discovered and proved.

36. Can Advanced Experience Be Popularized Effortlessly?

Page 461, paragraph 2, says, "In a socialist national economy science's latest achievements, technical inventions, and advanced experience can be popularized in all enterprises without the slightest difficulty." This is far from necessarily so. In a socialist society there are still "academic overlords" who control the organs of scientific research and repress new forces. This is why science's latest achievements are not simply popularized without the slightest difficulty. Such a manner of speaking essentially fails to recognize that there are contradictions within a socialist society. Whenever something new appears it is bound to meet with obstacles, perhaps because people are unaccustomed to it or do not understand it, or because it conflicts with the interests of a particular group. For example, our practices of close planting and deep furrowing have no class nature in and of themselves, yet they have been opposed and resisted by a particular group. Of course, in a socialist society such inhibiting conditions are fundamentally different from those in a capitalist society.

37. *Planning*

Page 465 quotes Engels as saying, "Under socialism it will become possible to carry out social production according to a predetermined plan." This is correct. In capitalist society equilibrium of the national economy is achieved through economic crises. In socialist society there is the possibility of making equilibrium a reality through planning. But let us not deny, because of this possibility, that knowledge of the required proportions must come through a process. Here the text says, "Spontaneity and *laissez faire* are incompatible with public ownership of the means of production." It should not be thought, however, that spontaneity and *laissez faire* do not exist in a socialist society. Our knowledge of the laws is not perfect all at once. Actual work tells us that in a given period of time there is such and such a plan by such and such people, or by a different group. No one can say that one particular group's plan conforms to the laws. Surely, some plans will accord or basically accord, while others will not or basically will not.

To think that knowledge of the proportions does not require a process—comparison between successes and failures, a tortuous course of development—is a metaphysical point of view. Freedom is the recognition of necessity, but necessity is not perceived in a glance. The world has no natural sages, nor upon attaining a socialist society does everyone become prescient. Why was not this text on political economy published at some earlier time? Why has it been revised time and again after its publication? And after all, is not the reason for this that knowledge was imperfect in the past and even now remains so? Take our own experiences—at the beginning we did not understand how to make socialism work; gradually, through practice, we came to understand a little, but not enough. If we think it is enough then nothing will be left to do!

On page 466 it says that an outstanding feature of socialism is "the conscious regular maintaining of due proportion."

This is both a responsibility and a demand, and a difficult one to fulfill. Even Stalin said that the plans of the Soviet Union could not be regarded as already fully reflecting what the laws demanded.

The "regular maintaining of due proportion" is at the same time the regular appearance of imbalances. For when due proportion is not achieved then the task of keeping things in proportion arises. In the course of the development of a socialist economy the regular appearance of imbalances requires us to balance things by holding to proportionality and comprehensiveness. For example, as the economy develops, shortages of technical personnel and cadres are felt all over, and a contradiction between needs and supply appears. This in turn spurs us to operate more schools and train more cadres to resolve this contradiction. It is after the appearance of imbalances and disproportion that people further understand the objective laws.

In planning, if no accounting is made, if we let things run their course, or are overly cautious insisting on everything being foolproof, then our methods will not succeed, and as a result proportionality will be destroyed.

A plan is an ideological form. Ideology is a reflection of realities, but it also acts upon realities. Our past plans stipulated that no new industry would be built on our coasts, and up to 1957 there was no construction there. We wasted seven years. Only after 1958 did major construction begin. These past two years have seen great developments. Thus, ideological forms such as plans have a great effect on economic development and its rate.

38. Priority Growth in Producing the Means of Production; Concurrent Promotion of Industry and Agriculture

On page 466 the problem of priority growth in producing the means of production is addressed.

Priority growth in producing the means of production is an economic rule for expanded reproduction common to all societies. If there are no priorities in producing the means of production in capitalist society there can be no expanded reproduction. In Stalin's time, due to special emphasis on priority development of heavy industry, agriculture was neglected in the plans. Eastern Europe has had similar problems in the past few years. Our approach has been to make priority development of heavy industry the condition for putting into effect concurrent promotion of industry and agriculture, as well as some other concurrent programs, each of which again has within it a leading aspect. If agriculture does not make gains few problems can be resolved. It has been four years now since we proposed concurrent promotion of industry and agriculture, though it was truly put into effect in 1960. How highly we regard agriculture is expressed by the quantity of steel materials we are allocating to agriculture. In 1959 we allocated only 590,000 tons but this year (including water conservancy construction) we allocated 1.3 million tons. This is truly concurrent promotion of industry and agriculture.

Here the text mentions that between 1925 and 1958 production of the means of production in the Soviet Union increased 103 times, while consumer goods increased 15.6 times. The question is, does a ratio of 103:15.6 benefit the development of heavy* industry or not? If we want heavy industry to develop quickly everyone has to show initiative and maintain high spirits. And if we want that then we must enable industry and agriculture to be concurrently promoted, and the same for light and heavy industry.

Provided that we enable agriculture, light industry, and heavy industry to develop at the same time and at a high rate, we may guarantee that the people's livelihood can be suitably improved together with the development of heavy industry. The experience of the Soviet Union, no less than our own, proves that if agriculture does not develop, if light industry does not develop, it hurts the development of heavy industry.

---

* Only in 1967 text.

39. *"Distribution Is Determinative"—An Erroneous View*

In chapter 20 it says, "The precondition for the high tide in state-managed industry was utilizing the workers' concern for their individual material interest in the development of socialist production." In chapter 21 it says, "Fully carry out economic accounting using the economic law of distribution according to labor (a law which combines workers' individual material interest with the interests of socialist production) to serve an important function in the struggle for national industrialization." In chapter 25 it says, "The goals of socialist production cause workers to be keenly concerned to make vigorous efforts to raise production and project personnel to be concerned with the fruits of their own labor, out of material interest. This is a powerful motive force for the development of socialist production." To make an absolute out of "concern for individual material interest" in this fashion is bound to entail the danger of increasing individualism.

Page 452 says that the law of distribution according to labor "is one of the determining motive forces for socialist production in that it causes all workers out of material interest to be concerned for the carrying out of plans to raise productivity." One cannot help asking, "If the fundamental economic laws of socialism determine the direction of development of socialist production, then how does it follow that individual material interest is alleged to be a determining motive force of production?" To treat distribution of consumer goods as a determining motive force is the erroneous view of distribution as determinative. Marx said, in his *Critique of the Gotha Programme,* "Distribution in the first place should be distribution of the means of production: in whose hands are the means of production? This is the determinative question. Distribution of the means of production is what determines distribution of consumer goods." To regard distribution of consumer goods as the determining motive force is a distortion of Marx's correct view and a serious theoretical error.

40. *Politics in Command and Material Incentive*

Page 452, paragraph 2, places party organization after local economic organs; these latter become the heads under the direct administration of the central government. Local party organizations cannot take the political lead in those areas, making it virtually impossible for them to mobilize all positive forces sufficiently. The text on page 457, although conceding the creative activities of the masses, nonetheless says, "One of the most important conditions for accelerating communist construction is the participation of the masses in the struggle to fulfill and overfulfill plans for national economic development." Page 447 also says, "Initiative of farm personnel is one decisive factor in developing agriculture." To regard the mass struggle as "one important factor" flies in the face of the principle that the masses are the creators of history. Under no circumstances can history be regarded as something the planners rather than the masses create.

Immediately afterward the text raises this point: "To begin with, we must utilize material incentives." This makes it seem as if the masses' creative activity has to be inspired by material interest. At every opportunity the text discusses individual material interest as if it were an attractive means for luring people into pleasant prospects. This is a reflection of the spiritual state of a good number of economic workers and leading personnel and of the failure to emphasize political-ideological work. Under such circumstances there is no alternative to relying on material incentives. "From each according to his ability, to each according to his labor." The first half of the slogan means that the very greatest effort must be expended in production. Why separate the two halves of the slogan and always speak onesidedly of material incentive? This kind of propoganda for material interest will make capitalism unbeatable!

41. Balance and Imbalance

Page 432, paragraph 1, is mistaken. The development of capitalist technology is balanced in certain respects, unbalanced
in others. The point is that balance and imbalance in technological development is essentially different under capitalism
and under socialism. Under socialism there is balance and
imbalance; for example, in the first period of Liberation we
had barely over 200 geological project workers, and prospect-
ing was altogether out of phase with the needs of the development of the national economy. After several years' intense
efforts the situation was practically rectified when fresh imbalances arose. At present there is in China an overwhelming
preponderance of manual labor, a situation quite out of phase
with our needs for developing production and raising labor
productivity. This is why we have to launch a broad technological revolution and resolve this imbalance. With the appearance of every new technical department imbalance of
technological development is bound to become noticeable
again. For example, we are now tackling higher technology
so we are conscious of the incompatibility of many things.
But this Soviet text not only denies a degree of balance under
capitalism but also a degree of imbalance under socialism.

Technology and the economy both develop in this way.
The text seems to be unacquainted with the wavelike advances of the development of socialist production and speaks
of the development of socialist economy as perfectly linear,
free of dips. This is unthinkable. No line of development is
straight; it is wave or spiral shaped. Even our studying has
this pattern. Before studying we do something else. Afterward we have to rest for a few hours. We cannot continue
studying as if there were neither day nor night. We study
more one day, less the next. Moreover in our daily study
sometimes we find more to comment upon, sometimes less.
These are all wavelike patterns, rising and falling. Balance is
relative to imbalance. Without imbalance there is no balance.
The development of all things is characterized by imbalance.

That is why there is a demand for balance. Contradiction between balance and imbalance exists in all parts of the various areas and departments, forever arising, forever being resolved. When there is a plan for the first year there has to be one for the next year as well. An annual plan requires a quarterly plan, which in turn requires a monthly plan. In every one of the twelve months contradictions between balance and imbalance have to be resolved. Plans constantly have to be revised precisely because new imbalances recur.

But the text has not adequately applied the dialectical method to research the various problems. The chapter devoted to the laws of planned proportional development of the national economy is quite long, yet no mention is made of the contradiction between balance and imbalance.

The national economy of a socialist society can have planned proportional development which enables imbalances to be regulated. However, imbalance does not go away. "Uneveness is in the nature of things." Because private ownership was eliminated it was possible to have planned organization of the economy. Therefore, it was possible to control and utilize consciously the objective laws of imbalance to create many relative temporary* balances.

If the productive forces run ahead, the production relations will not accord with the productive forces; the superstructure will not accord with the production relations. At that point the superstructure and the production relations will have to be changed to accord with the productive forces. Between superstructure and production relations, between production relations and productive forces—some say balance is only relatively attainable, for the productive forces are always advancing, therefore there is always imbalance. Balance and imbalance are two sides of a contradiction within which imbalance is absolute and balance relative. If this were not so, neither the superstructure nor the production relations, nor the productive forces, could further develop; they

---

* Only in the 1969 text.

would become petrified. Balance is relative, imbalance absolute. This is a universal law which I am convinced applies to
socialist society. Contradiction and struggle are absolutes;
unity, unanimity, and solidarity are transitional, hence relative. The various balances attained in planning are temporary, transitional, and conditional, hence relative. Who can
imagine a state of equilibrium that is unconditional, eternal?

We need to use balance and imbalance among the productive forces, the production relations, and the superstructure as a guideline for researching the economic problems of
socialism.

The main object of study in political economy is the production relations. But to study clearly the production relations it is necessary to study concomitantly the productive
forces and also the positive and negative effects of the superstructure on the production relations. The text refers to the
state but never studies it in depth. This is one omission. Of
course, in the process of studying political economy, the
study of the productive forces and the superstructure should
not become overdeveloped. If the study of the productive
forces goes too far it becomes technology and natural
science. If the study of the superstructure goes too far it
becomes nation-state theory, class struggle theory. Under the
heading of socialism (one of Marxism's three component
parts) what we study are: theories of class struggle, theories
of the state, theories of revolution and the party, as well as
military strategies and tactics, etc.

There is nothing in the world that cannot be analyzed.
But circumstances differ and so do essences. Many fundamental categories and laws—e.g., unity of contradiction—are applicable. If we study problems in this way, if
we observe problems in this way, we will then have a solid,
integral worldview and methodology.

---

42. *"Material Incentives"*

Page 486 says, "In the socialist stage labor has not yet become the primary necessity in the lives of all members of so-

ciety, and therefore material incentives to labor have the greatest significance." Here "all members" is too general. Lenin was a member of the society. Had *his* labor not become a "primary necessity" of his life?

Page 486 raises this point: there are two kinds of individuals in socialist society, the great majority who faithfully discharge their duties and the few who are dishonest about their duties. This is correctly analyzed. But if we want to bring around this latter group we can not rely exclusively on material incentives. We still have to criticize and educate them to raise their consciousness.

This section of the text speaks of workers who are comparatively diligent and positive. Conditions being equal, these are the ones who will produce more. Plainly, whether a worker is diligent and enthusiastic or not is determined by political consciousness, not by the level of technical or cultural expertise. Some whose technical and cultural level is high are nonetheless neither diligent nor enthusiastic; others whose level is lower are quite diligent and enthusiastic. The reason lies in the lower political consciousness of the former, the higher political consciousness of the latter.

The book says that material incentive to labor "spurs increases in production" and "is one of the decisive factors in stimulating the development of production." But material incentive does not necessarily change every year. People may not require such incentive daily, monthly, or yearly. In times of difficulty when incentives are reduced people must still carry on, and that satisfactorily. By making material incentive a onesided absolute the text fails to give due importance to raising consciousness, and cannot explain why there are differences among the labor of people in the same pay scale. For example, in scale no. 5,[22] one group may carry on very well, another rather poorly, and a third tolerably well on the whole. Why, with similar material incentive, such differences occur is inexplicable according to their way of reasoning.

Even if the importance of material incentive is recognized, it is never the sole principle. There is always another principle, namely, spiritual inspiration from political ideology.

And, while we are on the subject, material incentive can not simply be discussed as individual interest. There is also the collective interest to which individual interest should be subordinated, long-term interests to which temporary interests should be subordinated, and the interests of the whole to which partial interests should be subordinated.

In the section "Material Incentives to Labor, Socialist Emulation," there are some fairly well written passages concerning emulation. What is missing is the discussion of politics!

First, don't work people to death. Second, don't ruin their health, but even bring about gradual strengthening. These two points are basic. As for other things, if we can have them, fine, if not, well and good! We want the people to have some consciousness. The text seems to lay almost no emphasis on the future, the generations to come, only emphasizing material interest, constantly taking the road of material interest and rashly turning it into the principle of individual interest, as if it were a magic wand.

What they do not say is that individual interest will be satisfied when the interests of the whole people are satisfied. The individual material interest they emphasize is in reality myopic individualism, an economistic tendency from the period of proletarian class struggle against capitalism manifesting itself in the period of socialist construction. During the era of bourgeois revolutions a number of bourgeois revolutionaries made heroic sacrifices for the interests of their class and future generations of their class, but certainly not for immediate individual interest.

When we were in the base areas we had a free [nonmarket] supply system.[23] People were tougher then, and there was no wrangling at all on account of seeking preferential treatment. After liberation we had a wage system, and agreed upon scales, but our problems only multiplied. Many people wrangled frequently in a struggle for status, and we had to do a lot of persuading.

Our party has waged war for over twenty years without

letup. For a long time we made a nonmarket supply system work. Of course at that time the entire society of the base areas was not practicing the system. But those who made the system work in the civil war period reached a high of several hundred thousand, and at the lowest still numbered in the tens of thousands. In the War of Resistance Against Japan the number shot up again from over a million to several millions. Right up to the first stage of Liberation our people lived an egalitarian life, working hard and fighting bravely, without the least dependence on material incentives, only the inspiration of revolutionary spirit. At the end of the second period of the civil war we suffered a defeat, although we had victories before and after. This course of events had nothing at all to do with whether we had material incentives or not. It had to do with whether or not our political line and our military line were correct. These historical experiences have the greatest significance for solving our problems of socialist construction.

Chapter 26 says, "Workers in socialist enterprises who, out of material interest, are concerned with the results of their own work are the motive forces developing socialist production." (p. 482)

Chapter 27 says, "Compensation for skilled labor is comparatively high. . . . And this stimulates workers to raise their cultural and technical level, causing the essential difference between manual and mental labor to diminish." (pp. 501–03)

The point here is that higher compensation for skilled labor has spurred unskilled workers to upgrade themselves continuously so they can enter the ranks of skilled workers. This means that they studied culture and technology in order to earn more money. In a socialist society every person entering school to study culture and technology should recognize before anything else that they are studying for socialist construction, for industrialization, to serve the people, for the collective interest, and not above all for a higher wage.

Chapter 28 says, "Distribution according to labor is the

greatest force propelling the development of production." (p. 526) And at the end of this page, after explaining that wages rise steadily under socialism, the unrevised third edition of this textbook even goes so far as to say, "Socialism is fundamentally superior to capitalism precisely in this." Now to say that socialism is fundamentally superior to capitalism because wages steadily rise is very wrong. Wages are distribution of consumer goods. If there is no distribution of the means of production, there can be no distribution of the goods produced, of consumer goods. The latter is predicated on the former.

43. Interpersonal Relations in Socialist Enterprises

Page 500 says, "Under socialism the prestige of economic leaders is contingent upon the trust the masses have in them." This is well said indeed. But to reach this goal it will take work. In our experience, if cadres do not set aside their pretensions and identify with the workers, the workers will never look on the factory as their own but as the cadres'. "Master-of-the-house" attitudes make the workers reluctant to observe labor discipline in a self-conscious way. Do not think that under socialism creative cooperation between the workers and the leadership of the enterprises will emerge all by itself without the need to work at it.

If manual workers and enterprise leaders are both members of a unified production collective then "why do socialist enterprises have to put 'single leadership' into effect rather than leadership under collective guidance" i.e., the system of factory head responsibility under party committee guidance?

It is when politics is weakened that there is no choice but to talk about material incentive. That is why the text follows right up with "fully putting into effect the principle of having workers deeply concerned with the results of their own labor out of individual material interest is the mainspring for progressively grasping and raising socialist production."

44. Crash Programs, Accelerated Work

Page 505 says, "Do away with the phenomenon of accelerated work. Carry on production in a well-balanced way according to the blueprints." In the unrevised third edition this sentence reads, "We must fight against 'crash programs' and work in a well-balanced way according to predetermined schedules." This utter repudiation of crash programs and accelerated work is too absolute.

We can not completely repudiate crash programs. Their use or nonuse constitutes a unity of opposites. In nature there are gentle breezes and light rains, and there are high winds and violent rains. Use of crash programs appears and disappears, wavelike. In the technological revolution in production the need for them continually arises. In agriculture we must grapple with the seasons. The drama must have its climax. To gainsay crash programs is in reality to deny the climax. The Soviet Union wants to overtake the United States. We expect to reach the Soviet's level in less time than it took the Soviets. That is a kind of crash program.

Socialist emulation means that the backward overtakes the advanced. This is possible only through crash programs. Relations between individuals, between units, between enterprises, as well as between nations, are all competitive. If one wants to overtake the advanced, one cannot help having crash programs. If construction or revolution is attacked with executive orders (e.g., carrying out land reform or organizing cooperatives by administrative order) there is bound to be a reduction in production because the masses will not have been mobilized, and not because of crash programs.

45. The Law of Value and Planning

On page 521 there is a small print passage that is correct; it is critical, it joins the issues.

The law of value serves as an instrument of planning. Good. But the law of value should not be made the main basis of planning. We did not carry through the Great Leap on the basis of the demands of the law of value but on the basis of the fundamental economic laws of socialism and the need to expand production. If things are narrowly regarded from the point of view of the law of value the Great Leap would have to be judged not worth the losses and last year's all-out effort to produce steel and iron as wasted labor. The local steel produced was low in quantity and quality, and the state had to make good many losses. The economic results were not significant, etc. The partial short-term view is that the campaign was a loss, but the overall long-term view is that there was great value to the campaign because it opened wide a whole economic construction phase. Throughout the country many new starts in steel and iron were made, and many industrial centers were built. This enabled us to step up our pace greatly.

In the winter of 1959 over 75 million people were working on water conservancy nationwide. The method of organizing two large-scale campaigns could be used to solve our basic water conservancy problems. From the standpoint of one, two, or three years the value of the grain to pay for so much labor was naturally quite high. But in the longer view the campaign could considerably increase grain production and accelerate it too, and stabilize agricultural production, and so the value of commodities per unit gains. All this then goes toward satisfying the people's need for grain.

The continuing development of agriculture and light industry creates further accumulation for heavy industry. This too benefits people in the long run. So long as the peasants and the people of the entire country understand what the state is doing, whether money is gained or lost, they are bound to approve and not oppose. From among the peasants themselves the slogan of supporting industry has been put forward. There is the proof! Stalin as well as Lenin said, "In the period of socialist construction the peasantry must pay tribute to the state." The vast majority of China's peasants is "sending tribute" with a positive attitude. It is only among the prosperous peasants and the middle peasants, some 15 percent of the peasantry, that there is any discontent. They oppose the whole concept of the Great Leap and the people's communes.

In sum, we put plans ahead of prices. Of course we cannot ignore prices. A few years ago we raised the purchase price for live pigs, and this had a positive effect on pigbreeding. But for the kind of large-scale, nationwide breeding we have today, planning remains the main thing we rely on.

Page 521 refers to the problem of pricing in the markets of collective farms. Their collective farm markets have too much freedom. It is not enough to use only state economic power to adjust prices in such markets. Leadership and control are also necessary. In our markets, during the first stage, prices were kept within certain bounds by the government. Thus small liberties were kept from becoming big ones.

Page 522 says, "Thanks to our command of the law of value, the kind of anarchy in production or waste of social labor power the law entails under capitalism is not found in a socialist economy." This makes too much of the effects of the law of value. In socialist society crises do not occur, mainly because of the ownership system: the basic laws of socialism, national planning of production and distribution, the lack of free competition or anarchy, etc., and not because we command the law of value. The economic crises of capitalism, it goes without saying, are determined by the ownership system too.

46. Forms of Wages

Page 530, in its discussion of wage forms, advocates taking piecework wages as primary and the time-rate as supplementary. We do the reverse. Onesided emphasis on piece rates is bound to create contradictions between older and younger, stronger and weaker laborers, and will foster among the workers a psychology of "going for the big ones." This makes the primary concern not the collective cause but the individual income. There is even evidence that the piece-rate wage system impedes technological innovation and mechanization.

The book concedes that with automation, piece-rate wages are unsuitable. On the one hand they say they want automation widely developed; on the other they say they want piece-rate wages used widely. This involves a contradiction.

We have put into effect the time-rate system, plus rewards. The year-end "leap forward" bonuses of the last two years are an example. With the exception of governmental and educational workers, all staff and workers have had year-end leap forward bonuses in varying amounts determined by the staff and workers themselves in the particular units.

47. *Two Questions About Prices*

There are two questions that deserve study.

The first is the pricing of consumer goods. The text says, "Socialism has all along been putting into practice a policy of lowering the prices of consumer goods for the people." Our approach is to stabilize prices, generally neither letting them rise nor lowering them. Although our wage levels are comparatively low, universal employment and low prices and rents have kept the living standard of staff and workers decent enough. In the last analysis whether it is preferable to keep lowering prices or neither to raise nor lower them is a problem deserving study.

The other question concerns pricing of products of heavy and light industry. Relatively speaking, they have low prices for the former, and higher ones for the latter. We do the reverse. Why? Which is the better way in the last analysis is another problem deserving study.

PART III: CHAPTERS 30–34

48. *Concurrent Promotion of the Foreign and the Native, the Large, Medium, and Small*

Page 547 expresses opposition to dispersing construction funds. If they mean that not too many major projects should be undertaken at one time lest none can be completed on schedule, then of course we agree. But if the conclusion is to be that during major construction small- and medium-scale projects should be opposed, then we disagree. The principal new industrial centers in China were established on the basis of medium- and small-scale enterprises developed in large numbers in 1958. According to initial arrangements in the steel and iron industry, construction of twenty-nine large, nearly a hundred medium, and several hundred small-scale centers will be completed over the next eight years. The medium- and small-scale ones have already had a major effect on the steel and iron industry. Speaking from the standpoint of 1959, raw iron production nationwide has exceeded 20 million tons, half of which was produced by medium- and small-scale enterprises. In the future the medium- and the small-scale enterprise will continue to have major importance for the development of the steel and iron industry. Many small ones will become medium, many medium, large; backward ones will become advanced, local models will become like foreign ones—this is the objective law of development.

We will adopt advanced technology, but this cannot gainsay the necessity and the inevitability of backward technology for a period of time. Since history began, revolutionary wars have always been won by those whose weapons were deficient, lost by those with the advantage in weapons. During our civil war, our War of Resistance Against Japan, and our War of Liberation, we lacked nationwide political power and modernized arsenals. If one cannot fight unless one has the most modern weapons, that is the same as disarming one's self.

Our desire to make all-around mechanization such as the text describes a reality (p. 420) in our second decade appears still short of fulfillment; probably it will be in our third decade. In a future time, because of inadequate machinery, we will be calling for partial mechanization and improvement of our tools. For now we are holding off on general automation. Mechanization has to be discussed, but with a sense of proportion. If mechanization and automation are made too much of it is bound to make people despise partial mechanization and production by native methods. In the past we had such diversions, when everybody was demanding new technology, new machinery, the large scale, high standards; the native, the medium, or small in scale were held in contempt. We did not overcome this tendency until we promoted concurrently native *and* foreign, large *and* medium *and* small.

At the present time we have not proposed chemicalization of agriculture. One reason is that we do not expect to be able to produce much fertilizer in the next however many years. (And the little we have is concentrated on our industrial crops.) Another reason is that if the turn to chemicals is proposed everybody will focus on that and neglect pigbreeding. Inorganic fertilizers are also needed but they have to be combined with organic; alone they harden the soil.

The text speaks of adopting new techniques in every department. But this is not so easy to do. There must always be a process of gradual development. Moreover, even as some new machine is being adopted many old ones remain. The text is correct when it says that as you build new enterprises and renew equipment in existing factories, you should put existing machinery and mechanical equipment to use rationally and to the fullest extent. (p. 427) Things will be no different in the future.

As to the "large" and the "foreign," we must work on these in a spirit of "self reliance for new growth." In 1958 we proposed slogans on ridding ourselves of superstition and working with our own hands. The facts show that working on our own is quite feasible. In the past backward capitalist countries relied on the application of new techniques to catch up with advanced capitalist countries in production. The Soviet Union likewise relies on the application of advanced technology to catch up with the capitalist countries. We too must do the same, and we can.

49. Which First, Tractors or Cooperatives?

Page 563 says, "In 1928 on the even of overall collectivization, spring crop areas were tilled 99 percent with wood or horse-drawn ploughs." This fact refutes the text's repeated assertion that "tractors must precede cooperatives." On the same page we find, "Socialist production relations cleared a wide field for the development of agricultural productive forces and progress in agricultural technology." That is true.

First the production relations have to be changed, then and only then the productive forces can be broadly developed. This rule is universal. In some countries of Eastern Europe the cooperatives were not organized very energetically, and even today they remain uncompleted. The main reason is not that they lacked tractors (they had many more than we, comparatively speaking) but that their land reform was a top-down royal favor. Land was expropriated by quota (in some countries no expropriation was carried out on farms under 100 hectares); the work of expropriation was carried out by executive order; and after the land reform instead of striking while the iron was hot they let a full five or six years go by without doing much. We did quite the reverse. We put a mass line[24] into effect, roused the poor and lower-middle peasants to launch class struggle and seize all the land of the landlord class and distribute the surplus land of rich peasants, apportioning land on a per-capita basis. (This was a tremendous revolution in the rural areas.) Immediately afterward, we followed up with the mutual aid and cooperative movements. And from that point, steadily advancing step by step, we led the peasants on to the road to socialism. We had a massive party and army. When our forces went south a full complement of cadre squads had been set in place in every province to do local work at provincial, regional, county, and district levels. As soon as our forces would arrive they would penetrate deeply into the agricultural villages, "paying call on the poor to learn of their grievances," "striking roots and pulling things together," and getting the active elements of the poor and lower middle peasants organized.

50. Two Goals: Large and Public

The collective farms of the Soviet Union have undergone merger twice. Over 250,000 farms were merged into over 93,000, then these were again merged into about 70,000. In the future they will surely expand again. The text says (p. 568), "We must strengthen and develop the production relations of the various collective farms and organize publicly used production enterprises among the collective farms." Here, actually, there are many similarities to our own methods, they simply express things differently. In the future, even if their approach is like ours, it appears doubtful they will use the term *commune*. Differences in expression and terminology do include a substantive issue, namely, whether or not a mass line is being put into effect.

To be sure, the large scale of the Soviet Union's collective farms may never approach ours in terms of households and population because their rural population is sparse and their land area great. But who can say that for this reason their collective farms now need no further expansion? In places like Sinkiang and Ch'inghai the communes still need to enlarge even though there are few people for much land. Some counties in our southern provinces (e.g., northern Fukien) got large communes together under like conditions.

Enlarging the communes is a major issue. Changes in quantity are bound to bring on changes in quality, to stimulate such changes. Our people's communes are a good example—"Large! and Public!" First comes "Large!"—it will raise the level of "Public." This means that quantitative changes bring on partial qualitative changes.

51. What Is the Fundamental Reason for the Special Emphasis on Material Interest

In the chapter on the collective farm system there is continual discussion of individual material interest. (pp. 565, 571, etc.) The present special emphasis on material interest is for a reason. In the time of Stalin there was excessive emphasis on collective interest; individual gain was neglected. The public was overemphasized, the private underemphasized. Now they have gone to the opposite extreme, overemphasizing material incentive, neglecting collective interest. And if they persist in this course it will surely go to the opposite side again.

"Public" is in relation to "private," and vice-versa, a unity of opposites. One without the other is impossible. We have always spoken of joint consideration of public and private and long ago made the point that there is no such thing as all the one or the other, but that the public takes precedence over the private. The individual is a part of the collective. If the collective interest advances, the individual's lot will improve in consequence.

Duality is an attribute of all things, and for all time. Of course, duality is manifested through different concrete forms, and so the character of things varies. Heredity and mutation are a duality of opposites in unity. If there were only the latter without the former the succeeding generation would be utterly unlike the prior. Rice would no longer be that which makes it rice, nor dogs, nor people. The conservative side can have a good, a positive function. It can give living things in the midst of uninterrupted change a provisional constancy or stability. So, improved rice is still rice. But heredity without mutation would mean no advance, and development would come to a halt.

---

52. *It Is for the People to Act*

Page 577 says, "Collective farms offer the natural and economic conditions for allowing differential rent to be arranged." Differential rent is not altogether determined by objective conditions. Actually the matter rests with the people's doing. For example, in Hopei province there are many mechanized wells along the Peking-Hankow Railway, but very few along the Tientsin-Pukow. The natural conditions are similar, the communications equally convenient, but land improvements are never the same from place to place. There may have been reasons why the one locale was receptive (or unreceptive) to improvement, or there might have been varying historical reasons. But after all, the main thing is that it is for people to act.

While we are on the subject, some of the outlying districts of Shanghai are able to breed pigs properly, others not. In Ch'ung Ming county it was originally thought that certain natural conditions, e.g., the large number of lakes, would not be favorable for pigbreeding. But after getting rid of people's fears of difficulties, and after people adopted a positive attitude toward the business of breeding, it was realized that far from presenting an obstacle, these very natural conditions offered advantages. Actually, whether it is a matter of deep ploughing, fine horticulture, mechanization, or collectivization, it is for people to act.

Ch'ang P'ing county, Peking, has always been plagued by flood and drought. But things changed after the construction of the reservoir at the Ming Tombs. Does not this again illustrate that it is for people to act? In Honan they are planning after 1959 and 1960 to spend another three years to tame the Yellow River by completing construction of several large-scale conduits. All this shows again that it is for people to act.

53. Transport and Commerce

Transport and packaging do not increase use value, but they do increase value. The labor they use is a part of socially necessary labor. For without transportation and packaging the process of production would remain incomplete, would not enter the stage of consumption, and the use value produced could not be said to have been realized. Take coal. After the ore is mined, if it is left around the site and not delivered to the consumer by rail, steamer, or truck, its use value is completely unrealizable.

Page 585 says that they have two systems of commerce, state-operated and cooperative. In addition, they have "unorganized markets," i.e., the collective farm markets. We have only one system. We merged the cooperative trade into the state-operated trade, and the system now seems easy enough to run. There are lots of economies on all sides.

Page 587 refers to public supervision of commerce. For this we rely on party guidance in the main; with politics in command there is supervision by the masses. The labor of commercial workers is socially necessary and without it production cannot culminate in consumption (including productive consumption and individual consumption).

54. Concurrent Promotion of Industry and Agriculture

Page 623 discusses the rule of giving priority to increasing the means of production. The unrevised third edition mentions particularly here, "giving priority to increasing the means of production means that industry will develop at a faster rate than agriculture."

"Industry developing faster than agriculture" has to be posed in an appropriate way. One cannot emphasize industry to an inappropriate degree or trouble is sure to occur. Take our Liaoning: with its many industries, this province has an urban population that is one-third the total. In the past they had always put industry in first place, without attending at the same time to the vigorous development of agriculture. The result was that the province's agriculture could not guarantee supplies of grain, meats, and vegetables for the urban markets, and they always had to ship these items in from other provinces. The key issue is that agricultural labor is under great strain and is short of needed machinery. This limits the development of production; growth is comparatively slow. What we had failed to understand was that it was precisely in such places as the Northeast, particularly Liaoning, where we should have taken firm hold of agriculture. So one cannot emphasize only taking firm hold of industry.

Our position is that industry and agriculture should be developed together with priority given to developing heavy industry. The phrase "concurrent promotion" in no way denies priority in growth or faster development of industry than agriculture. At the same time, "concurrent promotion" is not equal utilization of our strength. For example, this year we estimate we can produce about 14 million tons of steel materials, of which 10 percent is to be applied to agricultural technological transformation and water conservancy construction. The remaining 90 percent is to be used mainly in heavy industry and communications and transportation construction. Under this year's conditions this is concurrent promotion of industry and agriculture. This should not be detrimental to priority growth of heavy industry or accelerating development of industry.*

Poland has 30 million people, but only 450,000 pigs. Now meat supplies are badly strained. Even today it would seem that Poland has not placed agricultural development on its agenda.

Page 624 says, "At different times it is necessary to accelerate the development of backward agriculture, light industry, and the food industry." Well and good, but imbalances and maladjustments created by backwardness in agriculture and light industry cannot be alleged to be merely "partial imbalances and maladjustments." These are questions of the totality.

Page 625 says, "Rational allocation of capital is necessary to maintain, at whatever time, correct proportions between heavy and light industry." This paragraph speaks only of heavy and light industry, not of industry and agriculture.

55. *Standards for Accumulation*

This has become a major issue in Poland. At the start Gomulka emphasized material incentive. He raised workers' wages but neglected to raise their consciousness, with the result that workers thought only of making more money but did not take the right spirit to their tasks. Increases of wages outstripped increases in productivity, and wages were eating up capital. The pressure has now forced them to come out in opposition to material incentive and to champion spiritual inspiration. Gomulka has even said, "Money cannot buy people's minds."

Overemphasis on material incentive always seems to lead to the opposite. Writing lots of checks naturally keeps the high-salary strata happy, but when the broad masses of work-

---

*Agriculture in the 1967 text.

ers and peasants want to cash in and find they cannot, the pressure to go to the "spiritual" is no surprise.

According to what is described on page 631, in the Soviet Union accumulated capital amounts to one-fourth of the national income. In China the figures were as follows: 27 percent in 1957, 36 percent in 1958, 42 percent in 1959, and it appears that in the future it will be possible to maintain regularly a figure of over thirty percent. The main problem lies in the vast development of production. Only if production increases and the percentages of accumulation go up a bit can people's livelihoods be finally improved.

It is our regular responsibility to practice economies and to accumulate large amounts of materials and wealth. It would be wrong to think that this should be done only in adverse conditions. It is difficult to believe that when hardships ease economies and accumulation are not needed.

PART IV: CHAPTER 35 TO THE CONCLUSION

56. *The Communist State*

Page 639 says, "In the higher stages of communism the state will become unnecessary and gradually diminish." Nonetheless this will require certain international conditions. If someone else has state machinery and you do not, it is dangerous. Page 640 says that even after communism is established, as long as imperialist countries exist, the state will continue to be necessary. This position is correct. Immediately after, the book says, "But the nature and the form of such a state will be determined by the particular features of the communist system." This sentence is hard to understand. The nature of the state is that it is a machinery for suppressing the opposed forces. Even if such a function is no longer needed internally, the coercive nature of the state will not have changed with respect to external opposing forces. The so-called form of the state means nothing more than armed forces, prisons, arrests, executions, etc. As long as imperialism still exists, what differences in form will there be when communism is reached?

57. *Transition to Communism*

Page 641 says, "In a socialist society there are no antagonistic classes," but "there are still vestiges of antagonistic classes." The transition from socialism to communism need not be made a reality through social revolution. All that can be said is that there is no need for a social revolution in which one class overthrows another, but there will be a social revolution in which new production relations and social institutions supersede old ones.

Here the text goes on to declare, "This certainly does not mean that society, as it develops along the road to communism, will not need to conquer internal contradictions." This declaration is merely incidental. Though there are places where this text recognizes contradictions, it does so only incidentally. One thing missing from this text is that it does not proceed from the analysis of contradictions in explaining issues. As a branch of science, political economy should begin its analysis with contradictions.

When a communist society is attained, labor discipline is bound to be even more strict than it is presently because the high level of automation will require ever higher exactitude of people's labor and conduct.

For now we are speaking of communist society as divided into two stages, a lower and a higher. This is what Marx and his circle foresaw based on conditions of social development at that time. After entering the higher stage communist society will develop into a new stage, and new goals and tasks will assuredly present themselves.

58. *The Future Development of Collective Ownership*

Page 650 says, "The production relations of the collective farms and the cooperatives have forms which accord fully with the present level and the present needs of the productive forces in the rural areas." I wonder if this is indeed true.

Introducing the Red October collective farm, a Soviet article says, "Before merger, some farms were difficult to manage in a good many respects. Afterward the problems cleared up." The article says that the farm has a population of ten thousand and that a housing project for three thousand residents is planned. This suggests that the present form of the farm is no longer fully compatible with the development of the productive forces.

The same passage says, "We must bend every effort to strengthening and further developing the cooperatives and the collective farm ownership system." If development is needed, a process has to be gone through, so why "bend every effort to strengthen?" Socialist production relations, social systems—of course one must speak in terms of consolidating them, but not to the point of ruining them. The text speaks vaguely of the road ahead, but the moment it comes to concrete measures it loses all clarity. In many ways (mainly production) the Soviets continue to progress, but with respect to the production relations fundamentally they have ceased to progress.

The text says that it is necessary to make a transition from collective ownership to indivisible ownership by the whole people. But from our point of view it is first necessary to turn collective ownership into socialist ownership by the whole people, i.e., to make the agricultural means of production entirely state owned, and to turn the peasants entirely into workers under uniform contract to the state for wages. At present, nationwide, each Chinese peasant has an average annual income of 85* yuan. In the future, when this amount will reach 150 yuan and the majority of workers are paid by the commune, it will be possible to make a commune ownership system basically work. In this way taking the next step to state ownership should be easy.

---

* 65 in the 1967 text.

59. Eliminating the Difference Between
Urban and Rural

The last paragraph on page 651 has a good position on rural construction.

Since they want to eliminate the difference (the book says "basic difference") between urban and rural, why does the text make a point of saying that it is not "to reduce the functions of the big cities?" The cities of the future need not be so large. Residents of large cities should be dispersed into the rural areas. Building many smaller cities is a relative advantage in case of nuclear war.

60. The Problem of the Various Socialist
Countries Setting Up an Economic System

Page 659 says, "Each country could concentrate its own manpower and material resources to develop its own most advantageous natural and economic conditions and departments with production experience and cadre. The respective countries would not need to produce goods which other countries could supply."

This is not a good idea. We do not suggest this even with respect to our own provinces. We advocate all-round development and do not think that each province need not produce goods which other provinces could supply. We want the various provinces to develop a variety of production to the fullest extent, provided there is no adverse effect on the whole. One of the advantages Europe enjoys is the independence of the various countries. Each is devoted to a set of activities, causing the European economy to develop comparatively quickly. Since the time of the Chin, China has taken shape as a major power, preserving its unity on the whole over a long period of time. One of the defects was bureaucratism, under the stifling control of which local regions could not develop independently, and with everyone temporizing, economic development was very slow. Now the situation is completely different. Within the unity we want to work toward, the various provinces will also have independence. This is relative unity and it is relative independence.

The provinces resolve their own problems independently while submitting to the resolutions of the central authorities and accepting their control. On the other hand, the center's resolutions on major issues are all made in common, through consultation between the center and the provinces. The resolutions of the Lushan Conference were like this, for example.[25] Not only did they accord with the needs of the whole country, they accorded with the needs of the various provinces. Who could take the position that only the center, not the localities, needs to oppose right opportunism? We champion having the provinces devote themselves fully to a set of activities under a unified plan for the whole country. Provided there are raw materials and markets, provided materials can be obtained and sales made locally, whatever can be done should be done to the fullest possible extent. Previously, our concern was that after the provinces had developed, a variety of industry, industrial goods (e.g., from a place like Shanghai) would in all likelihood not be wanted. Now it appears this is not the case. Shanghai has already proposed developing toward higher, larger scale, finer, and more excellent production. They still have things to do!

I wonder why the text fails to advocate each country's doing the utmost for itself rather than not producing goods which other countries could supply? The correct method is each doing the utmost for itself as a means toward self-reliance for new growth, working independently to the greatest possible extent, making a principle out of not relying on others, and not doing something only when it really and truly cannot be done. Above all, agriculture must be done well as far as possible. Reliance on other countries or provinces for food is most dangerous.

Some countries are so small that, exactly as the text says, "To develop all industrial departments would be economically irrational, a task to which their strength is unequal." In that case of course a country should not force it through. It would be very difficult for some of our own provinces with low population—Ch'inghai or Ninghsia—to have comprehensive development.

61. Can the Development of the Various Socialist Countries Be Evened Up?

Paragraph 3 on page 660 says, ". . . to have the overall level of economic and cultural development of the various socialist countries gradually draw parallel." The populations, resource bases, and historic conditions of these countries are not the same. Some of their revolutions were more backward, others more advanced. How can they be evened up? If a father has some dozen children, some tall, some short, some big some small, some bright, some slow, how can they be evened up? This is Bukharin's theory of balance. The economic development of the various socialist countries is not in balance, nor is that of the provinces within a country, or the counties within a province. Take public health in Kuangtung province. Fo Shan city and Chihlo commune have done a good job. Consequently Fo Shan is not in balance with the whole province. Chihlo is not in balance with Shaokuan. To oppose imbalances is wrong.

62. The Ultimate Question Is One of System

Page 668 says that socialist loans are different from imperialist loans. This tallies with the facts. Socialist countries are always preferable to capitalist ones. We understand this principle. The ultimate question is systemic, institutional. Systems determine the direction a country will take. Socialist systems determine that socialist countries will always stand opposed to imperialist countries and that their compromises are always provisional.

63. Relations Between the Two Economic Systems in the World

Page 658 speaks of "competition between the two world systems." In *Economic Problems of Socialism in the USSR,* Stalin offered arguments about the two world markets. The text here emphasizes peaceful competition between the two systems and building up "peacefully developing" economic relations. This turns the actually existing two world markets into two economic systems within a unified world market—a step back from Stalin's view.

Between the two economic systems there is in fact not only competition but also fierce, broad-ranging struggle, a struggle the text has kept its distance from.

64. Criticism of Stalin

Stalin's *Economic Problems of Socialism in the USSR,* like his other works, contains erroneous arguments. But the two accusations referred to on page 681 are not convincing.

One accusation is that Stalin held that "circulation of commodities seems to have already become an obstacle to the development of the productive forces. The necessity for gradually making the transition to direct exchanges of production between industry and agriculture is fully formed."

In this book Stalin said that when there are two kinds of ownership system then there is commodity production. He said that in the enterprises of the collective farms, although the means of production (land, tools, etc.) belong to the state, the goods produced are all the property of the separate collectives. The reason is that the labor on the collectives (like the seeds) is owned by the collectives, while the land that the state has given them for permanent use is in fact controlled by the collectives as if it were their own property. Under such conditions "the collective farms are willing to release into circulation what they produce only in the commodity form, in expectation of obtaining the commodities they need in exchange. At the present time the collective farms will not enter into any economic relations other than exchange through purchase and sales."

Stalin criticized the current view in the Soviet Union that advocated doing away with commodity production, holding that commodity production was no less necessary than it was thirty years earlier when Lenin declared the need for bending every effort to develop commodity circulation.

The text says that Stalin seemed to be advocating instant elimination of commodities. This accusation is difficult to make good. As to the question of commodity exchange, for Stalin it was only a hypothesis. For he had even said, "There is no need to promote this system with urgency; it must be decided according to the degree of accumulation of goods manufactured in the cities."

Another accusation is that Stalin underestimated the workings of the law of value in the sphere of production and especially with reference to the means of production. "In the sphere of socialist production the law of value plays no regulating role. This role is played by the law of planned proportional development and state planned economy." This argument offered by the text is in reality Stalin's own argument. Even though the text says that the means of production are commodities, nonetheless, in the first place, it must say that they are in the category of ownership by the whole people. Purchase and sale of the means of production in no way changes ownership. In the second place, the text ought to concede that the law of value functions differently in the sphere of production and in the process of circulation. All these arguments are consistent with Stalin's. One real difference between Stalin and Khrushchev is that Stalin opposed selling such means of production as tractors, etc. to the collective farms while Khrushchev sold them.

65. The Text's General Point of View

Do not think there is no Marxism-Leninism in this text, for it contains a good many views that are Marxist-Leninist. On the other hand, do not think it is entirely Marxist-Leninist, for it contains a good many views that deviate. We are not, however, ready to conclude that this text is basically negative.

The text emphasizes that a socialist economy serves the whole people, not the profit calculations of a minority of exploiters. The basic economic laws of socialism discussed in the text cannot be regarded as wholly in error. And these laws are the fundamental subject of the book. Also, the text explains planning, proportionality, high rate of development, etc., and in these respects is still socialist and Marxist. But once planning and proportionality are acknowledged, *how* these things are done is quite another matter. Each of us has his own approach.

Notwithstanding, this text has certain fundamental arguments that are in error. "Politics in command" and the "mass line" are not stressed. There is no discussion of "walking on two legs," and individual material interest is onesidedly emphasized. Material incentives are proclaimed and individualism is far too prominent.

In studying socialist economy the text does not proceed from contradictions. In truth, it does not acknowledge the universality of contradiction nor that social contradictions are the motive force of social development. The truth is that in their own society* there is still class struggle, that is, struggle between socialism and capitalist remnants. But this they do not concede. Their society* has three types of ownership: by the whole people, by the collective, and by the individual. Of course, such individual ownership is unlike individual ownership before collectivization, when the peasants' livelihood was entirely based on individual ownership. Now they have one foot on the boat and one still on shore, mainly relying on the collective but on the individual at the same time. If there are three types of ownership, there will be contradiction and struggle. But the text has no discussion of this. There is no encouraging of the mass movement. There is no

---

* Socialist society in the 1967 text.

acknowledgment of having collective ownership under socialism make the transition to public ownership under socialism, of turning the whole society into the indivisible possession of the whole people as a precondition for the transition to communism.

The text uses such vague terms as "rapprochement" and "concord" to take the place of the conception that one ownership system becomes another, one kind of production relations becomes another. In these respects the book has serious faults and serious errors and has partially deviated from Marxism-Leninism.

The text is very poorly written, neither persuasive nor interesting to read. It does not proceed from concrete analysis of the contradictions between the productive forces and the production relations nor the contradiction between the economic base and the superstructure. In posing questions, in researching problems, it always proceeds from general concepts or definitions. It gives definitions without making reasoned explanations. In fact, a definition should be the result, not the starting point, of an analysis. Quite without foundation the book offers a series of laws, laws which are not discovered and verified through analysis of concrete historical development. Laws cannot be self-explanatory. If one does not work from the concrete processes, the concrete historical development, laws will not be clearly explained.

The book does not deal with problems masterfully, with overall control of its subject. Issues do not stand forth clearly. The composition is not persuasive but is dull and illogical, lacking even formal logic. It appears as if written by different authors, each taking a chapter—a division of labor without unity. It lacks the systemic order a textbook should have. On top of this, its method is to proceed from definitions, and it reads like an economics dictionary. The authors are passive, contradicting one another in many places, later chapters at odds with earlier ones. Cooperative division of labor and collective authorship is one method. But the best method is to have one leader writing alongside of several assistants. This is the way Marx and his circle wrote, and their works were integral, and strictly, systematically scientific.

When writing the result will be exciting only if there is a target of criticism. Although this text has some correct things to say, it does not unfold a critique of views considered wrong. This makes the reading tedious.

In many places one feels as if a scholastic is speaking, not a revolutionary. The economist who does not understand economic practice is not a true expert. The book seems to reflect the following kind of situation: there are those who do practical work but lack the ability to generalize, as they lack concepts and laws; on the other hand, those who do theoretical work lack practical experience. These two types have not been integrated; that is, theory and practice have not been integrated.

The book shows that its authors do not have a dialectical method. One has to think philosophically to write an economics text. Philosophers should participate in the writing, otherwise it will not be possible to produce a satisfactory text.

The first edition of this text appeared in early 1955. But the basic framework seems to have been set even before then. And it looks as if the model Stalin set at that time was not very enlightening.

In the Soviet Union there are presently those who disagree with how the book was done. G. Kozlov wrote an article called "A Scientific Course of Study of Socialist Political Economy" which criticized this book. His views go to the root of the matter. He points out methodological faults of the book and calls for explanations of laws that proceed from an analysis of the process of socialist production. He also makes suggestions as to structure.

In view of the criticism of Kozlov and others it is possible that another textbook with an opposite approach will be produced in the Soviet Union. Opposition is always to the good.

From a first reading of this text one comes to realize its method and viewpoint. But that is not yet thorough study. What would be best in the future is to take the issues and arguments as the core, do some meticulous research, bring together some materials, and look over other available articles, books, reports, etc., with views that differ from those in this text. One should get an idea of the different opinions on controversial issues. To clarify issues the views of at least two sides have to be understood.

We must criticize and oppose wrong opinions, but we must also protect all correct things. Both courage and caution are needed.

No matter what, for them to have written a socialist political economy is a great task on the whole. Regardless how many problems it contains, this book at the least furnishes us with material for debate, and thanks to this has led to further study.

---

66. How to Write a Text on Political Economy

In principle it is permissible for the text to proceed from the ownership system. But there is an even better way. In researching the capitalist economy Marx, too, studied mainly ownership of the means of production under capitalism, examining how distribution of the means of production determined the distribution of commodities. In capitalist society the social nature of production and the private nature of ownership is a fundamental contradiction. Marx began with the commodity and went on to reveal the relations among people hidden behind commodities (the relations among things). Commodities in socialist society still have duality; nonetheless, thanks to the establishment of public ownership of the means of production and the fact that labor power is no longer a commodity, duality of commodities under socialism is not the same as their duality under capitalism. The relations among people are no longer hidden behind commodity relations. Thus, if socialist economy is studied beginning with the duality of commodities, copying Marx's method, it may well have the opposite effect of confusing the issues, making things harder for people to understand.

Political economy aims to study the production relations. As Stalin saw it, the production relations include three things: ownership, relations among people during labor, and the distribution of commodities. In writing a political economy of our own we could also begin with the ownership system. First, we describe the conversion of ownership of the means of production from private to public: how we converted private ownership of bureaucratic capital and the capitalist ownership system into socialist ownership by the whole people; how private ownership of the land by the landlords was turned first into private ownership by individual peasants and then into collective ownership under socialism; only then could we describe the contradiction between the two forms of public ownership under socialism and how collective ownership under socialism could make the transition to people's ownership under communism. At the same time, we must describe how people's ownership itself changes: the system of transferring cadres to lower levels, administration by different levels, right of autonomy of enterprises, etc. Although alike in being owned by the whole people, our enterprises are variously administered, some by departments of the center, others through provinces, municipalities, or autonomous regions, yet others through local special districts or counties. Some commune-run enterprises are semiowned by the whole people, semiowned by the collective. But whether centrally or locally administered, the enterprises are all under unified leadership and possess specific autonomous rights.

Turning to the problem of the relations among people during productive labor, the text, aside from such comments as "relations of comradely cooperation and mutual assistance," has completely failed to come to grips with the substantive issues, having conducted no research or analysis into this area. After the question of the ownership system is solved, the most important question is administration—how enterprises owned either by the whole people or the collective are administered. This is the same as the question of the relations among people under a given ownership system, a subject that could use many articles. Changes in the ownership system in a given period of time always have their limits, but the relations among people in productive labor may well, on the contrary, be in ceaseless change. With respect to administration of enterprises owned by the whole people, we have adopted a set of approaches: a combination of concentrated leadership and mass movement; combinations of party leaders, working masses, and technical personnel; cadres participating in production; workers participating in administration; steadily changing unreasonable regulations and institutional practices.

As to the distribution of commodities, the text has to be rewritten, changing its present approach altogether. Hard, bitter struggle, expanding reproduction, the future prospects of communism—these are what have to be emphasized, not individual material interest. The goal to lead people toward is not "one spouse, one country house, one automobile, one piano, one television." This is the road of serving the self, not the society. A "ten-thousand-league journey begins where you are standing." But if one looks only at the feet without giving thought to the future, then the question is: What is left of revolutionary excitement and ardor?*

---

67. How to Study Appearances to Reach Essences

In studying a problem one must begin with the appearances that people can see and feel, in order to research the essences that lie behind them, and then go on from there to reveal the substance and contradiction of objective things and events.

At the time of the civil war and the War of Resistance Against Japan our study of the problems of war proceeded from appearances. The enemy was big and strong, we were small and weak. This was the most obvious appearance at that time, one which all could see. We were the ones who studied and resolved problems, proceeding from appearances to study how the side which was small and weak might defeat an enemy which was big and strong. We pointed out that although we were small and weak we had mass support, and that the enemy, though big and strong, was vulnerable to

---

* "What energy is left for traveling?" in the 1967 text.

thrusts in certain areas. Take the civil war period, when the enemy had several hundred thousand men, we had several tens of thousands. Strategically, the enemy was strong and on the offensive, we were weak and on the defensive. But to attack us they had to divide their forces into columns, and the columns again into detachments. Typically, one company would attack a strong point while the others were still maneuvering. We would then concentrate several tens of thousands to attack one column, even concentrating the majority of our forces to take a single point of the enemy column, as another group would divert those enemy troops still maneuvering. In this way we achieved superiority at the particular point. The enemy had become small and weak, and we large and strong. Another thing is that when they would arrive at a place conditions would be unfamiliar to them, the masses would not support them, and so we would be able to wipe out an enemy group completely.

Ideology becomes systematic, generally speaking, in the wake of the movements of phenomena. The reason is that thought and understanding are reflections of material movements. Laws are things which appear over and over, not accidentally, in the movements of phenomena. It is only after the repeated appearance of something that it becomes a law and thus an object to be understood. For example, crises of capitalism occurred about every ten years. When this had happened over and over it then became possible for us to understand the laws of economic crisis in capitalist society. In land reform we had to distribute land according to population rather than labor power. But we did not understand this clearly until we had done it many times. In the late period of the second civil war "left" adventurist comrades called for distribution of land according to labor power and disapproved of distribution of land per capita. In their view even distribution of land according to population was not rigorous as to class outlook and not sufficiently from the outlook of the masses. Their slogan was: no land to the landlord, poor land to the rich peasant; to all others land according to labor power. Facts proved this approach to be wrong. How land should be distributed was made clear only after we had gone through experiences repeated over and over again

Marxism requires that logic be consistent with history. Thought is the reflex of objective existence. Logic comes from history. Though this textbook has an abundance of materials, there is no analysis, there is no logic, the laws are not discernible, and it is not satisfactory. But a lack of materials is also unsatisfactory. Then people will see only logic and not history. Moreover, it will be only subjective logic. Here exactly are the faults of this text.

It is vital to produce a history of the development of Chinese capitalism. If those who study history do not study the different societies, the different historical eras, they will surely be unable to produce good comprehensive histories. Studying the different societies means having to find the particular laws governing those societies. Once the particular laws have been studied and made clear, it will be easy to know the general laws of society. It is necessary to discern the general from the study of many particularities. If the particular laws are not understood clearly, the general cannot be either. For example, in studying the general laws governing animals it is necessary to study separately those governing vertebrates, invertebrates, etc.

68. Philosophy Must Serve the Political Tasks Facing Us

Any philosophy is in the service of its contemporary tasks.

Capitalist philosophy has this function. And every nation, every era has new theoreticians producing new theory for the political tasks of the day. In England such bourgeois materialists as Bacon and Hobbes appeared; materialists like the Encyclopedists then appeared in eighteenth-century France; the German and Russian bourgeoisie also had their materialists. All of these were bourgeois materialists, all of whom served the political tasks of the bourgeois class. Thus the existence of English or bourgeois materialism certainly did not make French bourgeois materialism unnecessary, nor did the existence of English and French bourgeois materialism make the German or the Russian unnecessary.

The Marxist philosophy of the proletarian class is even more vitally concerned to serve contemporary political tasks. For China, Marx, Lenin, and Stalin * are necessary reading. That comes first. But communists of any country and the proletarian philosophical circles of any country must create new theory, write new works, produce their own theoreticians to serve the political tasks facing them.

No nation can at any time rely only on what is old. Having Marx and Engels without Lenin's *Two Tactics* and other works could not have solved the new problems of 1905 and afterward. Having only *Materialism and Empirico-Criticism* of 1907 would not have sufficed to cope with the new issues that arose before and after the October Revolution. To meet the needs of this time Lenin wrote *Imperialism, State and Revolution* and other works. After Lenin, Stalin was needed to write *Foundations of Leninism* and *Problems of Leninism* to deal with reactionaries and preserve Leninism. At the end of our second civil war and the beginning of the War of Resistance Against Japan we wrote *On Practice* and *On Contradiction*. They had to be written to meet the needs of the times.

Now that we have entered the period of socialism a whole new series of problems has appeared. If we do not meet the new needs, write the new works, give form to new theory, it will not do!

SUPPLEMENT

1. *China's Industrialization Problems*

After the Soviet Union's first five-year plan had been completed, when the value of all large industrial production was 70 percent of the value of all industrial and agricultural pro-

---

* Omitted in the 1967 text.

duction, they promptly declared that industrialization had been made a reality. We too could quickly reach such a standard, but even if we did, we still would not claim that industrialization had become a reality, because we have over 500 million peasants devoting themselves to agriculture. If industrialization is claimed when industrial production is 70 percent, not only would we be unable to reflect accurately the actual conditions of our national economy, but we could even create a mood of laxity.

At the first plenary session of the Eighth National People's Congress we spoke of the necessity to establish a firm foundation for socialist industrialization in the second five-year plan. We also said that within fifteen years or so we would build an integrated industrial system. These two statements are somewhat contradictory, for without a fully equipped industrial system how can we speak of having a "firm foundation" for socialist industrialization? As things now stand, in another three years we may surpass England in output of primary industrial products. In another five years we can fulfill our task of establishing the industrial system as a practical reality.

In the long term, we expect to be known as an industrial-agricultural nation.* Even if we make over 100 million tons of steel it will still be so. If our per capita output were to surpass Great Britain's we would need to be producing 350 million tons of steel at least!

There is a special significance to picking out a country and competing with it. We are always talking about catching up with England. Our first step is to catch up in terms of primary product output, next in terms of per capita output. In shipbuilding and motor vehicle manufacture we are still far behind that country. We must strive to overtake it in all respects. Even so small a country as Japan has 4 million tons' capacity of commercial shipping. It is inexcusable for a country as large as ours to lack the shipping to move our own goods.

---

* ". . . we will not be known as an industrial nation" in the 1967 text.

In 1949 we had 90,000 or more sets of machine tools. By 1959 the number had increased to 490,000. In 1957 Japan had 600,000. The number of machine tools is an important index of the level of industrial development.

Our level of mechanization still is quite low, as one can tell simply from Shanghai, where, according to the most recent survey mechanized labor, semimechanized labor, and manual labor each constituted one-third.

Labor productivity in Soviet industry has not as yet surpassed that of the United States. We are even further behind. Though our population is very large our labor productivity is a long way from comparing with that of others. From 1960 on we will still have to work intensively for thirteen years.

---

2. Social Position and Individual Capacity

On page 488 it says that in a socialist society a person's position is determined only by labor and individual capacity. This is not necessarily so. Keen-minded people are always coming from among those in a lower position. They are looked down on by others, they have suffered indignities, and they are young. Socialist society is no exception. In the old society it was always the case that the oppressed had scant culture but were a bit keener; the oppressors had higher culture but were a little on the slow side. There is some danger of this today. The higher salaried strata of a socialist society have a bit more cultural knowledge but tend to be a trifle slow when compared to the lower strata. Thus our cadres' sons and daughters do not quite compare with the children of non-cadres.

From small plants have come many creations and discoveries. Larger factories may have superior facilities, newer technology, and for that very reason the staff all too often assume airs of self-importance, are satisfied with things as they are and do not seek to advance and reach out ambitiously. All too often their creativity does not compare at all with that of the staff of the smaller factory. Recently in Ch'angchou there was a textile mill in which the workers

created devices that raised the efficiency of the looms. This
will help cotton spinning, textile weaving, and printing and
dyeing achieve a balanced capability. The new technique did
not come from Shanghai or Tientsin but from a small place
called Ch'angchou.

Knowledge is gained by coming through adversity. If Ch'u
Yuan had remained in office his writings would not exist.[1]
Only because he lost his position and was "transferred down-
ward to perform labor" was it possible for him to get close to
the life of society and produce so fine a work of literature as
the *Li Sao*. And it was not until he had been rebuffed in
many states that Confucius also turned around and devoted
himself to his studies. He rallied a group of the unemployed
who expected to go from place to place to sell their labor
power. But no one would have them. Frustrated at every
turn, he had no alternative but to collect the folk songs now
known as the *Book of Odes* and put in order the historical
materials known as the *Spring and Autumn*.

Historically, many advanced things came not from advanced countries but from comparatively backward ones.
Marxism did not come from the comparatively developed capitalist countries of the time—England, France—but from Germany, whose level of capitalist development was in between.
There is a reason for this.

Scientific inventions likewise do not necessarily come
from those with a high level of culture and education. At
present there are many university professors who have not
invented anything. Of course, this is not to deny the difference between an engineer and a worker. It is not that we
do not want engineers. But there is a real question here. Historically it is usually a case of the culturally inferior defeating
the culturally superior. In our civil war our commanders at
various levels were culturally inferior to the Kuomintang officers, who came from military academies at home or abroad.
But we defeated them.

The human animal has this flaw: looking down on others.
Those who have accomplished some small thing look down
on those who have yet to. Great powers, rich nations look

down on the smaller, poorer ones. The Western nations looked down on Russia, historically. China is still in a similar position. There is reason for this, for we are still nothing much; such a large country, so little steel. So much illiteracy. It can do us good to have people look down on us! It will drive us to exert ourselves, to push forward.

3. Relying on the Masses

Lenin put it well when he said, "Socialism is vigorous, spirited, creative—the creation of the masses of the people themselves." Our mass line is like this. Does it not agree with Leninism? After quoting this statement the text says, "The broad laboring masses increasingly participate in a direct active way in the management of production, in the work of state bodies, in the leadership of all departments in the country's social life." (p. 332) This is also well put. But saying is one thing and doing another. And to do this is by no means easy.

In 1928 the Central Committee of the CPSU passed a resolution which said: "We will be able to solve the task of overtaking and surpassing the capitalist countries technically and economically only when the party and the worker and peasant masses get mobilized to the limit." (p. 337) This is very well put. And this is exactly what we are now doing. At that time Stalin had nothing else to rely on except the masses, so he demanded all-out mobilization of the party and the masses. Afterward, when they had realized some gains this way, they became less reliant on the masses.

Lenin said, "Truly democratic centralism requires that the manifold paths, forms, and methods by which local creativity and spirit of initiative attain general goals have a sufficiently unhindered development." (p. 454). Well said. The masses can create the paths. The masses created Russia's soviets. And they created our people's communes.

4. *The Soviet Union and China: A Few Points to Compare in the Development Process*

On page 422 the text quotes Lenin: "If state power is in the hands of the working class it is possible to make the transition to communism through state capitalism." And so forth. This is well put. Lenin was a solid worker. Because he realized that the proletariat after the October Revolution had no experience in managing the economy, he attempted to develop the proletariat's competence in this area by using the ways and means of state capitalism. The Russian bourgeoisie underestimated the strength of the proletariat at that time. Refusing Lenin's conditions, they carried out slowdowns and destructive activities, forcing the workers to confiscate their properties. That is why state capitalism could not develop.

During the civil war period Russia's problems were truly enormous. Agriculture was in ruins. Commercial links were disrupted. Communications and transport were hardly functioning. Raw materials could not be obtained, and many factories that had been expropriated could not commence operations. Because they really had no answer to this they had no choice but to turn to a system of requisitioning the peasants' surplus grain. Actually, this was a means of taking the fruits of the peasants' labor without compensation, a method that meant ransacking the jars and boxes of the peasants—not a sound practice. Only when the civil war ended was this system replaced with a grain tax.

Our civil war lasted much longer than theirs. For twenty-two years it was our practice in the base areas to collect public grain and to purchase surplus grain. We had a correct strategy toward the peasanty and during the war we relied heavily on them.

For twenty-two years we developed our political power in the base areas, and we accumulated experience in managing the economy of the base areas. We trained cadres to manage the economy and built an alliance with the peasantry, so that after the whole country was liberated we speedily carried to its completion the work of economic recovery. Immediately after that we raised the general line of the transition period, namely, putting our primary effort into socialist revolution while beginning construction under the first five-year plan. As we carried out socialist transformation we worked together with the peasantry to deal with the capitalists. There was, however, a time when Lenin said that he could bear to negotiate even with the capitalists in hopes of turning capitalism into state capitalism as a means of coping with the spontaneity of the petty bourgeoisie. Different policies arise in different historical conditions.

In the New Economic Policy (NEP) period the Soviet Union had a restrained policy toward the rich peasants because they needed the grain. We had a similar policy toward the national bourgeoisie in the early stages after liberation. Not until the collective farms and the state farms had produced in all 400 million pood of grain did they move against the rich peasants, putting forward the slogan of eliminating the rich peasants and making overall collectivization a reality.* What about us? We did things differently, actually eliminating the rich peasant economy as early as land reform.

In the Soviet Union cooperative movement "agriculture paid a heavy price at the beginning." (p. 397) This is what caused many of the East European countries to have plenty of anxiety over the question of cooperativization and to be

---

* In "Several Questions Concerning Soviet Land Policy" (December 1929) Stalin said, "In 1927 the rich peasants produced over 600 million pood of grain, of which 130 million were sold through rural exchange. This is a substantial force which we can not slight. Tell me, how much had our collective and state farms produced at that time? About 80 million pood, of which 30 million were commodity grains." So Stalin decided, "Under these circumstances we can not resolutely attack the rich peasants." And Stalin continued, "Now we have a sufficient material basis to attack them." That was because in 1929 the collective and state farms produced no less than 400 million pood, of which over 130 million were commodity grains. (Josef Stalin, *Complete Works,* vol 12, p. 142)

fearful of organizing big. When they did get started they moved slowly. Our production was not reduced by the cooperatives. On the contrary, it increased enormously. At the beginning many were dubious. Now the number of converts is slowly increasing.

5. *The Process of Forming and Consolidating a General Line*

These past two years we have been conducting a great experiment.

In the early stages of Liberation we had no experience of managing the economy of the entire nation. So in the period of the first five-year plan we could do no more than copy the Soviet Union's methods, although we never felt altogether satisfied about it. In 1955, when we had basically completed the "three transformations"[2] (at the end of the year and in the spring of the following year), we sought out over thirty cadres for consultation. As a result of those discussions we proposed the "ten great relationships" and "More! Faster! Better! More economically!" At that time we had read Stalin's 1949 election speech, which stated that tsarist Russia was producing 4 million tons of steel annually. The figure increases to 18 million by 1940. If one reckons from 1921, there is an increase of only 14 million tons in twenty years. And to think they were socialist the whole time! Could we not do a little better, faster? After that we put forward the question of "two methods" and at the same time we worked out a forty-article program for agricultural development.[3] No other measures were proposed at the time.

After the forward leap of 1956, opposition to* adventurous advances appeared. Bourgeois rightists took us by our pigtails and attacked savagely in an attempt to negate the accomplishment of socialist construction. In June 1957, at the National People's Congress, Premier Chou En-lai's report struck back at the rightists. In September the same year the party's

---

*Only in the 1967 text.

third plenary session of the Central Committee revived such slogans as "More! Faster! Better! More economically!" the general program in forty articles, the society for the promoting of progress,* etc. In November in Moscow we revised a *People's Daily* editorial on "More! Faster! Better! More economically!" Thus, in the winter we launched a nationwide mass movement for large-scale water conservancy.

In 1958 there were meetings, first in Nanning, then in Ch'engtu. We tore into our problems, criticizing those opposed to daring advances. We decided not to allow further opposition to daring advances. We proposed a general line for socialist construction. If there had been no Nanning meeting we could not have come up with a general line. In May a representative† of the Central Committee reported to the Eighth National People's Congress, second session. And the assembly officially passed the general line. But the line was not consolidated, so we followed with concrete measures, mainly concerning division of authority between the center and the local areas. In Peitaiho we proposed doubling steel output and got a mass movement in steel and iron underway—what the Western papers called backyard steel. At the same time we launched the people's communes. Right after came the shelling of Quemoy. These things perturbed some and offended others. Errors appeared in our work. By not paying for food we ate ourselves into a crisis in grains and nonstaple foods. The ultracommunist wind was blowing. A certain percent‡ of daily necessities could not be supplied. Steel output for 1959 was set at 30 million tons at Peitaiho. The Wuchang meeting lowered this to 20 million. The Shanghai meeting lowered it to 16.5 million tons. Sometime in June 1959 it was cut again to 13 million. All this was seized upon by those who disagreed with us. But when the Central Committee was opposing the "left" they did not raise their objections, nor did they do so at the two Ch'engchou

---

* "Great Leap Forward" in the 1967 text.
† Liu Shao-Ch'i in the 1967 text.
‡ 12 percent in the 1967 text.

conferences, the Wuchang Conference, the Peking Conference, or the Shanghai Conference. They waited until the "left" had been opposed out of existence and goals had been confirmed. Further opposition to the "left" made opposition to the right necessary. At the Lushan Conference, when we needed opposition to the right, they came out against the "left."[4]

All this goes to show that things were far from peaceful in our world, and the general line was certainly not consolidated. Now that we have come through a period of difficult zigzags and the Lushan Conference, the general line is comparatively consolidated. But "things come in threes," so perhaps we have to prepare for a third period of zigzags. If so, we can expect that the line will be consolidated even further. According to Chekiang Provincial Committee information "equalization" and "indiscriminate transfers of property" have reappeared very recently in certain communes. The ultracommunist wind may yet appear again!

The incidents in Poland and Hungary occured in 1956, the time of the zigzags of the campaign against "daring advances." Then the world turned against the Soviet Union. During the zigzags of 1959 the world turned against us.

The two rectification and antirightist campaigns, one in 1957, one at Lushan, subjected the effects of bourgeois ideology and remaining bourgeois influences to comparatively throughgoing criticism, enabling the masses to be liberated from the danger. At that time we also struck down many superstitions, including the so-called Ma Anshan Iron and Steel Constitution.*[5]

In the past we did not know how to get a socialist revolution going. We thought that after the cooperatives, after joint public-private management, the problem would be solved. The savage attacks of the bourgeois rightists caused us to put forward socialist revolution as a political and an ideological line. Actually, the Lushan Conference carried forward this revolution, and it was a sharp revolution. It would have been

---

*"An authoritarian refining method at a major Soviet mill"—note in the 1967 text.

very bad if we had not beaten down the right opportunist line at Lushan.

6. Contradictions Among the Imperialist Nations and Other Matters

Struggles among the respective imperialisms should be seen as a major thing. That is how Lenin saw them and Stalin too, something they called the indirect reserve force of the revolution. In getting the revolutionary base areas going China enjoyed this advantageous circumstance. In the past we had contradictions among various factions of the landlord and compradore classes. Behind these domestic contradictions lay contradictions among the imperialists. It was because of these contradictions among the imperialists that only a part of the enemy rather than all of them would do battle with us directly in a particular time, so long as we utilized the contradictions properly. In addition, we usually had time to rest and reorganize.

Contradictions among the imperialists was one important reason why the October Revolution could be consolidated. Fourteen nations sent intervention forces at the time. But none alone sent much. Moreover, their purposes were not co-ordinated. They were engaged in intrigues. During the Korean war American purposes were not coordinated with those of their allies. The war was not fought on the largest scale. Not only could America not determine its own course, France and England were not so eager.

Internationally the bourgeoisie are now extremely uneasy, afraid of any wind that might stir the grass. Their level of alertness is high, but they are in disarray.

Since the Second World War the economic crises in capitalist society are different from those of Marx's day. Generally speaking, they used to come every seven, eight or ten years. During the fourteen years between the end of the Second World War and 1959 there were three.

At present the international scene is far more tense than after the First World War, when capitalism still had a period of relative stability, the revolution having failed everywhere except Russia. England and France were full of high spirits and the various national bourgeoisies were not all that afraid of the Soviet Union. Aside from the taking away of Germany's colonies the entire imperialist colonial system was still in tact. After the Second World War three of the defeated imperialisms collapsed. England and France were weakened and in decline. Socialist revolution had triumphed in over ten countries. The colonial system was breaking apart. The capitalist world would never again enjoy the relative stability it had after the First World War.

7. Why China's Industrial Revolution Can Be Very Rapid

In Western bourgeois public opinion there are now those who acknowledge that "China is one of the countries having the most rapid industrial development." (The U.S. Conlon report on United States diplomatic policy mentions this.)

There are many countries that have carried through an industrial revolution. Compared to all previous national industrial revolutions China promises to have one of the most rapid.

The question is, why? One of the main reasons is that our socialist revolution was carried through fairly thoroughly. We carried through the revolution against the bourgeoisie thoroughly, doing our utmost to eradicate all bourgeois influences. We struck down superstitions and energetically sought to enable the masses to win thoroughgoing liberation in all areas.

8. Population *

In eliminating the problem of excess population, rural population is the major problem, the solution of which calls for vast development of production. In China over 500 million people are devoting themselves to agriculture. But they do

---

* This section is found in the 1969 text only.

not eat their fill, although they toil year in year out. This is most unreasonable. In America the agricultural population is only 13 percent and on the average each person has 2,000 catties[6] of grain. We do not have so much. What shall we do to reduce the rural population? If we do not want them crowding into the cities we will have to have a great deal of industry in the countryside so that the peasants can become workers right where they are. This brings us to a major policy issue: do we want to keep rural living conditions from falling below that in the cities, keep the two roughly the same, or keep the rural slightly higher than the urban? Every commune has to have its own economic center, its own upper-level schools to train its own intellectuals. There is no other way to solve the problem of excess rural population really and truly.

Concerning
Economic Problems of Socialism in the USSR
(November 1958)[1]

Provincial and regional committees must study this book. In
the past everyone read it without gaining a deep impression.
It should be studied in conjunction with China's actual circumstances. The first three chapters contain much that is
worth paying attention to, much that is correct, although
there are places where perhaps Stalin himself did not make
things clear enough. For example, in chapter 1 he says only a
few things about objective laws and how to go about planning the economy, without unfolding his ideas; or, it may be
that to his mind Soviet planning of the economy already reflected objective governing principles. On the question of
heavy industry, light industry, and agriculture, the Soviet
Union did not lay enough emphasis on the latter two and had
losses as a result. In addition, they did not do a good job of
combining the immediate and the long-term interests of the
people. In the main they walked on one leg. Comparing the
planning, which of us after all had the better adapted
"planned proportionate development?" Another point: Stalin
emphasized only technology, technical cadre. He wanted
nothing but technology, nothing but cadre; no politics, no
masses. This too is walking on one leg! And in industry they
walk on one leg when they pay attention to heavy industry
but not to light industry. Furthermore, they did not point out
the main aspects of the contradictions in the relationships
among departments of heavy industry. They exaggerated the
importance of heavy industry, claiming that steel was the

foundation, machinery the heart and soul. Our position is that grain is the mainstay of agriculture, steel of industry, and that if steel is taken as the mainstay, then once we have the raw material the machine industry will follow along. Stalin raised questions in chapter 1: he suggested the objective governing principles, but he failed to provide satisfactory answers.

In chapter 2 he discusses commodities, in chapter 3 the law of value. Relatively speaking, I favor many of the views expressed. To divide production into two major departments and to say that the means of production are not commodities—these points deserve study. In Chinese agriculture there are still many means of production that should be commodities. My view is that the last of the three appended letters* is entirely wrong. It expresses a deep uneasiness, a belief that the peasantry cannot be trusted to release agricultural machinery but would hang on to it. On the one hand Stalin says that the means of production belong to state ownership. On the other, he says that the peasants cannot afford them. The fact is that he is deceiving himself. The state controlled the peasantry very, very tightly, inflexibly. For the two transitions Stalin failed to find the proper ways and means, a vexing matter for him.

Capitalism leaves behind it the commodity form, which we must still retain for the time being. Commodity exchange laws governing value play no regulating role in our production. This role is played by planning, by the great leap forward under planning, by politics-in-command. Stalin speaks only of the production relations, not of the superstructure, nor of the relationship between superstructure and economic base. Chinese cadres participate in production; workers participate in management. Sending cadres down to lower levels to be tempered, discarding old rules and regulations—all these pertain to the superstructure, to ideology. Stalin mentions economics only, not politics. He may speak of selfless

---

* Reply to Comrades A. V. Sanina and V. G. Venzher, included in *Economic Problems*.

labor, but in reality even an extra hour's labor is begrudged. There is no selflessness at all. The role of people, the role of the laborer—these are not mentioned. If there were no communist movement it is hard to imagine making the transition to communism. "All people are for me, I for all people." This does not belong. It ends up with everything being connected to the self. Some say Marx said it. If he did let's not make propaganda out of it. "All people for me," means everybody for me, the individual. "I am for all." Well, how many can you be for?

Bourgeois right is manifested as bourgeois law and education. We want to destroy a part of the ideology of bourgeois right, the lordly pose, the three styles [the bureaucratic, the sectarian, and the subjective] and the five airs[the officious, the arrogant, the apathetic, the extravagant, and the precious]. But commodity circulation, the commodity form, the law of value, these, on the other hand, cannot be destroyed summarily, despite the fact that they are bourgeois categories. If we now carry on propaganda for the total elimination of the ideology of bourgeois right it would not be a reasonable position, bear in mind.

There are a few in socialist society—landlords, rich peasants, right-wingers—who are partial to capitalism and advocate it. But the vast majority are thinking of crossing over to communism. This, however, has to be done by steps. You cannot get to heaven in one step. Take the people's communes: on the one hand, they have to develop self-sufficient production, on the other, commodity exchange. We use commodity exchange and the law of value as tools for the benefit of developing production and facilitating the transition. We are a nation whose commodity production is very underdeveloped. Last year we produced 3.7 trillion catties of foodgrains. Of that number, commodity grains amounted to about 800 or 900 billion catties. Apart from grain, industrial crops like cotton and hemp are also underdeveloped. Therefore we have to have this [commodity] stage of development. At present there are still a good many counties where there is no charge for food but they cannot pay wages. In Hopei there are three such counties, and another that can pay wages, but not much: three or five yuan. So we still have to develop production, to develop things that can be sold other than foodgrains. At the Sian Agricultural Conference this point was insufficiently considered. In sum, we are a nation whose commerce is underdeveloped, and yet in many respects we have entered socialism. We must eliminate a part of bourgeois right, but commodity production and exchange must still be kept. Now there is a tendency to feel that the sooner communism comes the better. Some suggest that in only three or five years we will be making the transition. In Fan county, Shantung, it was suggested that four years might be a little slow!

At present there are some economists who do not enjoy economics—Yaroshenko* for one. For now and until some time in the future we will have to expand allocation and delivery to the communes. And we will have to expand commodity production. Otherwise we will not be able to pay wages or improve life. Some of our comrades are guilty of a misapprehension when, coming upon commodities and commodity production, they want to destroy bourgeois rule every single day, e.g., they say wages, grades, etc., are detrimental to the free supply system. In 1953 we changed the free supply system into a wage system.[2] This approach was basically correct. We had to take one step backward. But there was a problem: we also took a step backward in the matter of grades. As a result there was a furor over this matter. After a period of rectification grades were scaled down. The grade system is a father-son relation, a cat-and-mouse relation. It has to be attacked day after day. Sending down the cadres to lower levels, running the experimental fields[3]— these are ways of changing the grade system; otherwise, no great leaps!

In urban people's communes capitalists can enter and serve as personnel. But the capitalist label should stay on them. With respect to socialism and communism, what is meant by constructing socialism? We raise two points:

---

* Recipient of Stalin's second letter, included in *Economic Problems*.

(1) The concentrated manifestation of constructing socialism is making socialist, all-embracing public ownership* a reality. (2) Constructing socialism means turning commune collective ownership into public ownership. Some comrades disapprove of drawing the line between these two types of ownership system, as if the communes were completely publicly owned. In reality there are two systems. One type is public ownership, as in the Anshan Iron and Steel Works, the other is commune-large collective ownership. If we do not raise this, what is the use of socialist construction? Stalin drew the line when he spoke of three conditions. These three basic conditions make sense and may be summarized as follows: increase social output; raise collective ownership to public ownership; go from exchange of commodities to exchange of products, from exchange value to use value.

On these two abovementioned points we Chinese are (1) expanding and striving to increase output, concurrently promoting industry and agriculture with preference given to developing heavy industry; and (2) raising small collective ownership to public ownership, and then further to all-embracing public ownership. Those who would not draw these distinctions [among types of ownership] would seem to hold the view that we have already arrived at public ownership. This is wrong. Stalin was speaking of culture when he proposed the three conditions, the physical development and education of the whole people. For this he proposed four conditions: (a) six hours' work per day; (b) combining technical education with work; (c) improving residential conditions; (d) raising wages. Raising wages and lowering prices are particularly helpful here, but the political conditions are missing.

All these conditions are basically to increase production. Once output is plentiful it will be easier to solve the problem of raising collective to public ownership. To increase production we need "More! Faster! Better! More economically!" And for this we need politics-in-command, the four concurrent promotions, the rectification campaigns, the smashing of the ideology of bourgeois right. Add to this the people's com-

---

*This is identical, in Chinese, to ownership by the whole people.

munes and it becomes all the easier to achieve "More! Faster! Better! More economically!"

What are the implications of all-embracing public ownership? There are two: (1) the society's means of production are owned by the whole people; and (2) the society's output is owned by the whole people.

The characteristic of the people's commune is that it is the basic level at which industry, agriculture, the military, education, and commerce are to be integrated in our social structure. At the present time it is the basic-level administrative organization. The militia deals with foreign threats, especially from the imperialists. The commune is the best organizational form for carrying out the two transitions, from socialist (the present) to all-embracing public, and from all-embracing public to communist ownership. In future, when the transitions have been completed, the commune will be the basic mechanism of communist society.

Critique of Stalin's *Economic Problems of Socialism in the USSR*

Stalin's book from first to last says nothing about the super-structure. It is not concerned with people; it considers things, not people. Does the kind of supply system for consumer goods help spur economic development or not? He should have touched on this at the least. Is it better to have commodity production or is it better not to? Everyone has to study this. Stalin's point of view in his last letter* is almost altogether wrong. The basic error is mistrust of the peasants.

Parts of the first, second, and third chapters are correct; other parts could have been clearer. For example, the discussion on planned economy is not complete. The rate of development of the Soviet economy is not high enough, although it is faster than the capitalists' rate. Relations between agriculture and industry, as well as between light and heavy industry, are not clearly explained.

It looks as if they have had serious losses. The relationship between long- and short-term interests has not seen any spectacular developments. They walk on one leg, we walk on two. They believe that technology decides everything, that cadres decide everything, speaking only of "expert," never of "red," only of the cadres, never of the masses. This is walking on one leg. As far as heavy industry goes, they have failed to find the primary contradiction, calling steel the foundation, machinery the heart and innards, coal

---

* Reply to comrades A. V. Sanina and V. G. Venzher.

the food. . . . For us steel is the mainstay, the primary contradiction in industry, while foodgrains are the mainstay in
agriculture. Other things develop proportionally.

In the first chapter he discusses grasping the laws, but
without proposing a method. On commodity production and
the law of value he has a number of views that we approve of
ourselves, but there are problems as well. Limiting commodity production to the means of subsistence is really rather
doubtful. Mistrust of the peasants is the basic viewpoint of
the third letter. Essentially, Stalin did not discover a way to
make the transition from collective to public ownership.
Commodity production and exchange are forms we have
kept, while in connection with the law of value we must
speak of planning and at the same time politics-in-command.
They speak only of the production relations, not of the superstructure nor politics, nor the role of the people. Communism
cannot be reached unless there is a communist movement.*

> 1. These comrades . . . it is evident . . . confuse laws of
> science, which reflect objective processes in nature or society,
> processes which take place independently of the will of man,
> with the laws which are issued by governments, which are
> made by the will of man, and which have only juridical validity.
> But they must not be confused.

1. This principle is basically correct, but two things are
wrong: first, the conscious activity of the party and the
masses is not sufficiently brought out; second, it is not comprehensive enough in that it fails to explain that what makes
government decrees correct is not only that they emerge
from the will of the working class but also the fact that they
faithfully reflect the imperatives of objective economic laws.

> 2. Leaving aside astronomical, geological, and other similar
> processes, which man really is powerless to influence, even if
> he has come to know the laws of their development. . . .

---

* These first four paragraphs comment critically on the entire text. There
follows a series of comments criticizing specific sections. Before each comment Stalin's original text is given, as translated for *Jen min ch'u pan she,*
3rd ed., January 1938. (We use the English edition of Foreign Languages
Press, Peking, 1972).

2. This argument is wrong. Human knowledge and the capability to transform nature have no limit. Stalin did not consider these matters developmentally. What cannot now be done, may be done in the future.

3. The same must be said of the laws of economic development, the laws of political economy—whether in the period of capitalism or in the period of socialism. Here, too, the laws of economic development, as in the case of natural science, are objective laws, reflecting processes of economic development which take place independently of the will of man.

3. How do we go about planning the economy? There is not enough attention given to light industry, to agriculture.

4. That is why Engels says in the same book: "The laws of his own social action, hitherto standing face to face with man as laws of nature foreign to, and dominating, him, will then be used with full understanding, and so mastered by him." (*Anti-Dühring*)

4. Freedom is necessary objective law understood by people. Such law confronts people, is independent of them. But once people understand it, they can control it.

5. The specific role of Soviet government was due to two circumstances: first, that what Soviet government had to do was not to replace one form of exploitation by another, as was the case in earlier revolutions, but to abolish exploitation altogether; second, that in view of the absence in the country of any ready-made rudiments of a socialist economy, it had to create new, socialist forms of economy, "starting from scratch," so to speak.

5. The inevitability of socialist economic laws—that is something that needs to be studied. At the Ch'engtu Conference I said that we would have to see whether or not our general program ("More! Faster! Better! More economically!" the three concurrent promotions, and the mass line) would flop; [1] or if it could succeed. This can not be demonstrated for several or even as many as ten years. The laws of the revolution, which used to be doubted by some, have now been proved correct because the enemy has been overthrown. Can socialist construction work? People still have doubts. Does

our Chinese practice conform to the economic laws of China?
This has to be studied. My view is that if the practice conforms generally, things will be all right.

6. This [creating new, socialist forms of economy "from
scratch"] was undoubtedly a difficult, complex, and unprece-
dented task.

6. With respect to the creating of socialist economic
forms we have the precedent of the Soviet Union and for this
reason should do a bit better than they. If we ruin things it
will show that Chinese Marxism does not work. As to the difficulty and complexity of the tasks, things are no different
from what the Soviet Union faced.

7. It is said that the necessity for balanced (proportionate) development of the national economy in our country enables the
Soviet government to abolish existing economic laws and to
create new ones. That is absolutely untrue. Our yearly and five-
yearly plans must not be confused with the objective economic
law of balanced, proportionate development of the national
economy.

7. This is the crux of the matter.

8. That means that the law of balanced development of the national economy makes it *possible* for our planning bodies to plan
social production correctly. But *possibility* must not be confused with *actuality*. They are two different things. In order to
turn the possibility into actuality, it is necessary to study this
economic law, to master it, to learn to apply it with full understanding, and to compile such plans as fully reflect the requirements of this law. It cannot be said that the requirements of
this economic law are fully reflected by our yearly and five-
yearly plans.

8. The central point of this passage is that we must not
confuse the objective law of planned proportionate development with planning. In the past we too devised plans, but
they frequently caused a storm. Too much! Too little! Blindly
we bumped into things, never sure of the best way. Only
after suffering tortuous lessons, moving in U-shaped pat-

terns, everyone racking their brains to think of answers, did we hit upon the forty-article agricultural program which we are now putting into effect. And we are in the midst of devising a new forty articles. After another three years' bitter struggle we will develop further; after full and sufficient discussions we will again proceed. Can we make it a reality? It remains to be proved in objective practice. We worked on industry for eight years but did not realize that we had to take steel as the mainstay. This was the principal aspect of the contradiction in industry. It was monism. Among the large, the medium, and the small, we take the large as the mainstay; between the center and the regions, the center. Of the two sides of any contradiction one is the principal side. As important as eight years' achievements are, we were feeling our way along, nonetheless. It cannot be said that our planning of production was entirely correct, that it entirely reflected the objective laws. Planning is done by the whole party, not simply the planning committee or the economics committee, but by all levels; everyone is involved. In this passage Stalin is theoretically correct. But there is not yet a finely detailed analysis, nor even the beginnings of a clear explanation. The Soviets did not distinguish among the large, the medium, and the small, the region and the center; nor did they promote concurrently industry and agriculture. They have not walked on two legs at all. Their rules and regulations hamstrung people. But we have not adequately studied and grasped our situation, and as a result our plans have not fully reflected objective laws either.

9. Let us examine Engels' formula. Engels' formula cannot be considered fully clear and precise, because it does not indicate whether it is referring to the seizure by society of *all* or only part of the means of production; that is, whether *all* or only part of the means of production are converted into public property. Hence, *this* formula of Engels' may be understood either way.

9. This analysis touches the essentials! The problem is dividing the means of production into two parts. To say the means of production are not commodities deserves study.

10. In this section, Commodity Production Under Social- ism, Stalin has not comprehensively set forth the conditions for the existence of commodities. The existence of two kinds of ownership is the main premise for commodity production. But ultimately commodity production is also related to the productive forces. For this reason, even under completely so- cialized public ownership, commodity exchange will still have to be operative in some areas.

> 11. It follows from this that Engels has in mind countries where capitalism and the concentration of production have ad- vanced far enough both in industry and agriculture to permit the expropriation of *all* the means of production in the country and their conversion into public property. Engels, consequently, considers that in *such* countries, parallel with the socialization of *all* the means of production, commodity production should be put an end to. And that, of course, is correct.

11. Stalin's analysis of Engels' formula is correct. At present there is a strong tendency to do away with commod- ity production. People get upset the minute they see com- modity production, taking it for capitalism itself. But it looks as if commodity production will have to be greatly developed and the money supply increased for the sake of the solidarity of several hundred million peasants. This poses a problem for the ideology of several hundred thousand cadres as well as for the solidarity of several hundred million peasants. We now possess only a part of the means of production. But it ap- pears that there are those who wish to declare at once owner- ship by the whole people, divesting the small and medium producers. But they fail to declare the category of ownership! Is it to be commune-owned or county-owned? To abolish commodities and commodity production in this way, merely by declaring public ownership, is to strip the peasantry. At the end of 1955, procurement and purchase got us almost 90 billion catties of grain, causing us no little trouble. Everyone was talking about food, and household after household was talking about unified purchase. But it was purchase, after all, not allocation. Only later did the crisis ease when we made

the decision to make this 83 billion catties of grain. I cannot understand why people have forgotten these things so promptly.

12. I leave aside in this instance the question of the importance of foreign trade to Britain and the vast part it plays in her national economy. I think that only after an investigation of this question can it be finally decided what would be the future [fate] of commodity production in Britain after the proletariat had assumed power and *all* the means of production had been nationalized.

12. Fate depends on whether or not commodity production is abolished.

13. But here is a question: What are the proletariat and its party to do in countries, ours being a case in point, where the conditions are favorable for the assumption of power by the proletariat and the overthrow of capitalism [where capitalism has so concentrated the means of production in industry that they may be expropriated and made the property of society, but where agriculture, notwithstanding the growth of capitalism, is divided up among numerous small and medium owner-producers to such an extent as to make it impossible to consider the expropriation of these producers?] * . . . [This] would throw the peasantry into the camp of the enemies of the proletariat for a long time.

13. In sum, the principle governing commodity production was not grasped. Chinese economists are Marxist-Leninist as far as book learning goes. But when they encounter economic practice Marxism-Leninism gets shortchanged. Their thinking is confused. If we make mistakes we will lead the peasantry to the enemy side.

14. Lenin's answer may be briefly summed up as follows: (a). Favorable conditions for the assumption of power should not be missed—the proletariat should assume power without waiting until capitalism has succeeded in ruining the millions of small and medium individual producers;

---

* Material in brackets added from Stalin's text to clarify the point.

15(b). The means of production in industry should be expropriated and converted into public property;

16(c). As to the small and medium individual producers, they should be gradually united in producers' cooperatives, i.e., in large agricultural enterprises, collective farms;

17(d). Industry should be developed to the utmost and the collective farms should be placed on the modern technical basis of large-scale production, not expropriating them, but on the contrary generously supplying them with first-class tractors and other machines;

18(e). In order to ensure an economic bond between town and country, between industry and agriculture, commodity production (exchange through purchase and sale) should be preserved for a certain period, it being the form of economic tie with the town which is *alone acceptable* to the peasants, and Soviet trade—state, cooperative, and collective-farm—should be developed to the full and the capitalists of all types and descriptions ousted from trading activity.

The history of socialist construction in our country has shown that this path of development, mapped out by Lenin, has fully justified itself.

19. There can be no doubt that in the case of all capitalist countries with a more or less numerous class of small and medium producers, this path of development is the only possible and expedient one for the victory of socialism.

14. This passage has a correct analysis. Take conditions in China. There is development. These five points are all correct.

15. Our policy toward the national bourgeoisie has been to redeem their property.

16. We are developing the people's communes on an ever larger scale.

17. This is precisely what we are doing now.

18. There are those who want no commodity production, but they are wrong. On commodity production we still have to take it from Stalin, who, in turn, got it from Lenin. Lenin had said to devote the fullest energies to developing com-

merce. We would rather say, devote the fullest energies to developing industry, agriculture, and commerce. The essence of the problem is the peasant question. There are those who regard the peasant as even more conscious than the workers. We have carried through or are in the process of carrying through on these five items. Some areas still have to be developed, such as commune-run industry or concurrent promotion of industry and agriculture.

19. Lenin said the same thing.

20. Commodity production must not be regarded as something sufficient unto itself, something independent of the surrounding economic conditions. Commodity production is older than capitalist production. It existed in slave-owning society, and served it, but did not lead to capitalism. It existed in feudal society and served it, yet, although it prepared some of the conditions for capitalist production, it did not lead to capitalism.

21. Bearing in mind that in our country commodity production is not so boundless and all-embracing as it is under capitalist

22. conditions, being confined within strict bounds thanks to such decisive economic conditions as social ownership of the means of production, the abolition of the system of wage labor, and the elimination of the

23. system of exploitation, why then, one asks, cannot commodity production similarly serve our socialist society for a certain period without leading to capitalism?

20. This statement is a little exaggerated. But it is true that commodity production was not a capitalist institution exclusively.

21. The second plenary session of the Central Committee suggested policies of utilizing, restricting, and transforming (commodity production.)

22. This condition is fully operative in China.

23. This point is entirely correct. We no longer have such circumstances and conditions. There are those who fear commodities. Without exception they fear capitalism, not realizing that with the elimination of capitalists it is allowable to expand commodity production vastly. We are still backward

in commodity production, behind Brazil and India. Commodity production is not an isolated thing. Look at the context: capitalism or socialism. In a capitalist context it is capitalist commodity production. In a socialist context it is socialist commodity production. Commodity production has existed since ancient times. Buying and selling began in what history calls the Shang ["commerce"] dynasty. The last king of the Shang dynasty, Chou, was competent in civil and military matters, but he was turned into a villain along with the first emperor of the Ch'in[2] and Ts'ao Ts'ao.[3] This is wrong. "Better to have no books than complete faith in them."[*] In capitalist society there are no socialist institutions considered as social institutions, but the working class and socialist ideology do exist in capitalist society. The thing that determines commodity production is the surrounding economic conditions. The question is, can commodity production be regarded as a useful instrument for furthering socialist production? I think commodity production will serve socialism quite tamely. This can be discussed among the cadres.

24. It is said that, since the domination of social ownership of the means of production has been established in our country, and the system of wage labor and exploitation has been abolished, commodity production has lost all meaning and should therefore be done away with.

24. Change "our country" to "China" and it becomes most intriguing.

25. Today there are two basic forms of socialist production in our country: state, or publicly owned production, and collective-farm production, which cannot be said to be publicly owned.

25. "Today" refers to 1952, thirty-five years after their revolution. We stand but nine years from ours.

He refers to two basic forms. In the communes not only land and machinery but labor, seeds, and other means of production as well are commune-owned. Thus the output is

---

[*] Mencius. Mao seems to mean "Let's not make a stock villain out of commodity production pedantically."

so owned. But don't think the Chinese peasants are so wonderfully advanced. In Hsiuwu county, Honan, the party secretary was concerned whether or not, in the event of flood or famine, the state would pay wages after public ownership was declared and the free supply system instituted. He was also concerned that in times of bumper harvest the state would transfer away public grain but not pay wages either, leaving the peasants to suffer whether the harvest succeeds or fails. This represents the concerns of the peasants. Marxists should be concerned with these problems. Our commodity production should be developed to the fullest, but it is going to take fifteen years or more and patience as well. We have waged war for decades. Now we still have to have patience, to wait for Taiwan's liberation, to wait for socialist construction to be going well. Don't hope for early victories!

26. [How the two basic forms of ownership will ultimately become one] is a special question which requires separate discussion.

26. Stalin is avoiding the issue, having failed to find a method or suitable formulation [on the transition from collective to public ownership.]

27. Consequently, *our* commodity production is not of the ordinary type, but is a special kind of commodity production, commodity production without capitalists, which is concerned mainly with the goods of associated socialist producers (the state, the collective farms, the cooperatives), the sphere of action of which is confined to items of personal consumption, which obviously cannot possibly develop into capitalist production, and which, together with its "money economy," is designed to serve the development and consolidation of socialist production.

27. The "sphere of action" is not limited to items of individual consumption. Some means of production have to be classed as commodities. If agricultural output consists of commodities but industrial output does not, then how is exchange going to be carried out? If "our country" is changed to "China," the paragraph becomes all the more interesting to

read. In China not only consumer goods but agricultural means of production have to be supplied. Stalin never sold means of production to the peasants. Khrushchev changed that.

28. (Chairman Mao commented on page 13 of the original text): Let us not confuse the problem of the dividing line between socialism and communism with the problem of the dividing line between collective and public ownership. The collective ownership system leaves us with the problem of commodity production, the goal of which is consolidating the worker-peasant alliance and developing production. Today there are those who say that the communism of the peasants is glorious. After one trip to the rural areas they think the peasantry is simply wonderful, that they are about to enter paradise, that they are better than the workers. This is the surface phenomenon. We shall have to see if the peasants really have a communist spirit, and more than that, we shall have to examine the commune ownership system, including the extent to which the means of production and subsistence belong to communal collective ownership. As the county party committee secretary of Hsiuwu, Honan, said, we still have to develop commodity production, and not charge blindly ahead.

29. Further, I think that we must also discard certain other concepts taken from Marx's *Capital*—where Marx was concerned with an analysis of capitalism—and artificially applied to our socialist relations. . . . It is natural that Marx used concepts (categories) which fully corresponded to capitalist relations. But it is strange, to say the

30. least, to use these concepts now, when the working class is not only not bereft of power and means of production, but, on the contrary, is in possession of the power

31. and controls the means of production. Talk of labor power being a commodity, and of "hiring" of workers sounds rather absurd now, under our system, as though the working class, which possesses means of production, hires itself and sells its labor power to itself.

29. In particular, the means of production in the industrial sector.

30. Commodity production has to be vastly developed, not for profits but for the peasantry, the agricultural-industrial alliance, and the development of production.

31. Especially after rectification. After the rectification and anti-rightist campaigns labor power was no longer a commodity. It was in the service of the people, not the dollar. The labor power question is not resolved until labor power is no longer a commodity.

32. It is sometimes asked whether the law of value exists and operates in our country, under the socialist system.

32. The law of value does not have a regulative function. Planning and politics-in-command play that role.

33. True, the law of value has no regulating function in our socialist production.

33. In our society the law of value has no regulative function, that is, has no determinative function. Planning determines production, e.g., for hogs or steel we do not use the law of value; we rely on planning.

Notes

Reading Notes

1. There are three levels of collective ownership in the Chinese countryside. The smallest unit, the production team, usually consists of between fifteen and thirty-five families. The team is the basic ownership and production unit, owning the land it works, a number of draught animals, and small agricultural tools such as threshers and crushers. The next unit, the production brigade, is made up of from five to fifteen teams. The brigade owns larger means of production too expensive for the team to buy and too large for them to use effectively, such as tractors and irrigation equipment. The brigade also takes care of tasks, such as hill terracing, for which the team is too small. The commune, with a population from several thousand to some fifty thousand, is composed of ten to thirty brigades. In addition to providing overall coordination among the brigades, the communes own and run large industrial enterprises and projects too large for the brigade to handle, such as large water conservancy projects.

2. The various forms of collective ownership, taken as a whole, are distinct from ownership by the whole people. Collective ownership signifies that the means of production are owned by a sector of the total population. This sector, be it a team, brigade, or commune, basically organizes and runs production. The product of a collectively owned unit, aside from taxes, belongs to the units which produced it. The unit uses part of the product for reproduction and investment and the remainder for worker income.

    Ownership by the whole people, on the other hand, signifies

149

ownership by the whole society, not a sector of it. Such enterprises are subject to direct central planning and organization. Their products are owned by the whole society and can be distributed according to need within the whole system of units under ownership by the whole people. Since these various production units are treated as a unified accounting unit, the profits or losses of an individual production unit do not affect either investment in the unit or the income of its workers.

In 1973, industry under the ownership of the whole people accounted for 97 percent of total fixed assets, 63 percent of the people engaged in industry, and 86 percent of total industrial output. Industry under collective ownership covered 3 percent of fixed assets, 36.2 percent of the industrial workforce, and 14 percent of total output. Individual handicrafts made up the other 8 percent. In commerce, 92.5 percent of retail sales were under ownership of the whole people with collectively owned units accounting for 7.3 percent of total retail sales. In agriculture, on the other hand, 80 to 90 percent of the means of production were still under collective ownership.

3. The land reform movement refers specifically to the post-Liberation land reform campaign of 1949–1952. The agricultural producers' cooperatives were established for the most part during the high tide of collectivization in 1955 and early 1956. The people's communes were organized throughout China in the fall of 1958 during the initial stages of the Great Leap Forward.

4. Compradore capitalism refers to foreign commercial establishments in China staffed by Chinese who served these foreign interests.

5. For Mao's discussions of the importance of bureaucratic capital and policy toward it at that time, see "The Present Situation and Our Tasks," December 25, 1947, and "Report to the Second Session of the Seventh Central Committee," March 5, 1949, in *Selected Works of Mao Tsetung,* vol. 4 (Peking: Foreign Languages Press, 1961), pp. 167–68 and 362–75.

6. Here Mao is referring to the activities of Chang Po-chün (Zhang Po-jun) and Lo Lung-chi (Luo Long-ji). In the summer of 1957 Chang suggested giving more power to the Chinese People's Political Consultative Conference, which consisted largely of members of the various democratic parties. This unit would serve as an "upper house" with veto power over the CCP-

dominated National People's Congress. Lo proposed a set of "rehabilitation committees" to examine the treatment of democratic persons who he argued were unfairly treated in the anti-counter-revolutionary campaigns of the early 1950s.

7. Fixed interest was a specific part of the CCP's strategy of "buying out" the national bourgeoisie. After Liberation, policy toward them went through several stages. The first stage was the placing of orders by the state with private enterprises for manufacturing and processing and the unified purchase and distribution of products produced by these enterprises. After the rectification campaign in private industry in 1952, a second phase of "dividing the profits into four shares" was implemented. The four relatively equal shares were: (1) taxes paid to the state; (2) contributions to the worker welfare fund; (3) enterprise development funds; and (4) profits for the capitalists.

The third stage was the implementation of joint state-private ownership, first of individual enterprises and then of entire trades. In this "highest phase of state capitalism," the income of the capitalists would come from the income they received for the work they did within the units and from "fixed interest." Fixed interest was to be paid for twenty years at the annual rate of 5 percent of the value of the assets of the enterprises regardless of the annual profits or losses of the individual firms. Fixed interest payments were terminated during the Cultural Revolution.

8. The policy of unified purchase and supply meant that the government would buy certain products at fixed prices, thus eliminating the private market and conditions for speculation in these goods. Unified purchase and supply of grain, edible oils, and oilseeds was instituted in March 1954, and in September 1954 the policy was instituted for cotton and cotton cloth.

Under the system of unified purchase and supply, there are three categories of goods. Goods in the first category (which, as of April 1959, included 38 products) are sold to state companies at fixed prices. Second category goods (293 products as of April 1959) are sold to the state according to quotas reached on a contractual basis. Above-quota production can, but need not, be sold to the state. Third category goods (those not included in the first or second categories) may still be sold on the market.

9. "Red and expert" describes a unity of opposites in building a socialist society. Redness suggests political and ideological

aspects of work; expertness the technical aspects. Both are necessary aspects of all work. But in line with his reasoning that every contradiction must have a primary aspect, Mao has long held that "ideological and political work is the guarantee . . . the 'soul' " of economic and technical work. On the other hand, if redness is emphasized to the exclusion of expertness, then the unity of opposites will be destroyed and the task of building socialism will become impossible.

10. In March 1949 the CCP began to organize a People's Political Consultative Conference representing twenty-three parties and groups. In September 1949 the Preparatory Committee of the People's Political Consultative Conference met and passed the Common Program, a general statement of the aims of the new government, and the Organic Law of the Central People's Republic which made the working class the leaders of the Republic. Subsequently, the National People's Congress, first convened in 1954, was established as the dominant long-term national legislative body in China.

11. One Chinese dollar (yuan) has a value of U.S. $.53 (April 1977). The value of the yuan has been stable at approximately U.S. $.50 for over twenty years, the variations coming mainly as a result of devaluations of the U.S. dollar.

12. Here Mao is probably referring to his own experiences during the Great Leap Forward. At Wuchang (Wuzhang) in November 1958, Mao admitted that at the Peitaiho (Beitaihe) Conference in August 1958, during the height of enthusiasm for the Great Leap, he had made a similar error of considering only need and not capacity.

13. This formulation of these crucial contradictions is contained in Mao's April 1956 speech, "On the Ten Major Relationships."

14. Mutual aid teams were an early form of collective agricultural organization. Based on traditional peasant seasonal labor-sharing practices in parts of China, they were extensively implemented in the early 1950s. In 1955, nearly 60 percent of China's peasant households were in mutual aid teams.

These teams were supplanted in 1955 by elementary agricultural producers' cooperatives (APCs). Each APC contained several mutual aid teams; land and other capital goods continued to be privately owned, but other resources were pooled and used according to annual plans prepared by cooperative decision-making.

By June 1956, however, 63 percent of the peasant house-holds had progressed to larger, advanced APCs in which land, labor, and the means of production were pooled.

15. Chang Tien-p'ei (Zhung Dian-pei) was a film critic in the mid-1950s who later took part in the antiparty, antisocialist current of 1957.

16. The "three-antis" (Sanfan) campaign, begun in the northeast in August 1951 and nationally in January 1952, was directed against corruption, waste, and bureaucratism among government employees, many of whom were still carryovers from the Nationalist regime. The "five-antis" (Wufan) campaign was directed at the national bourgeoisie. Its specific foci were the elimination of bribery, theft of state property, tax evasion, theft of state economic secrets, and embezzlement in carrying out government contracts.

17. Here Mao is referring to the rightist criticisms of the CCP during the "blooming and contending" period in the spring of 1957, shortly after he had delivered his talk, "On the Correct Handling of Contradictions Among the People," in February 1957.

18. In July 1959, at the Lushan Conference, a group of party leaders headed by then Defense Minister P'eng Teh-huai (Peng De-huai) criticized the Great Leap Forward and its leadership as "petty bourgeois fanaticism." They argued that it had created far more damage than good. After a major struggle at the plenum conference, P'eng and other rightists were removed from their positions of responsibility in the party and the government.

19. The argument presented by the textbook that the socialist revolution in the ideological and political fronts was concluded in 1957 is similar to the argument in the Resolution of the Eighth Party Congress in 1956. That is to say, the main contradiction in China was no longer that between the bourgeoisie and the proletariat, but between the advanced relations of production (the ideological and political fronts on which the revolution was "concluded") and the backward forces of production.

20. The 45 percent rate of accumulation noted here by Mao is an exceptionally high one used to demonstrate an exemplary advanced situation. During the Great Leap Forward, Mao had consistently argued against excessive rates of accumulation which would reduce the peasants' incentives to produce. As a general rule, he prescribed the following breakdown for agricultural production: taxes (7 percent); production expenses (20

percent); accumulation (18 percent); distribution to the masses (55 percent).

21. The Eight-Character Charter for Agriculture, propagated during the Great Leap Forward, called for paying attention to water, fertilizer, soil (conservation), seeds (selection), closeness (in planting), protection (of plants), implements, and (field) management.

22. Here Mao is referring to the fifth grade in China's present eight-grade wage system.

23. During the War of Liberation, cadres received goods according to need, not according to work done. These goods were distributed directly for use, not through any market mechanism based on exchange value. Under these circumstances, however, needs were defined quite spartanly.

24. The mass line is the method of leadership which the CCP strives to achieve. Its classic formulation by Mao is as follows:

> In all the practical work of our Party, all correct leadership is necessarily "from the masses, to the masses." This means: take the ideas of the masses (scattered and unsystematic ideas) and concentrate them (through study turn them into concentrated and systematic ideas), then go to the masses and propagate and explain these ideas until the masses embrace them as their own, hold fast to them, and translate them into action, and test the correctness of these ideas in such action. Then once again concentrate ideas from the masses and once again go to the masses so that the ideas are persevered in and carried through. And so on, over and over again in an endless spiral, with the ideas becoming more correct, more vital, and richer each time.

From: "Some Questions Concerning Methods of Leadership," June 1, 1943, *Selected Works,* vol. 3, p. 119.

25. Mao is referring again to the July-August 1959 Lushan Conference at which the conflict with P'eng Teh-huai came to the fore.

Supplement

1. Ch'u Yuan (Qu Yuan) was an aristocrat of the Chou period who lived during the beginning of the third century B.C. After being dismissed from the royal court, he wrote the *Li Sao,* an allegori-

cal, fanciful search for an understanding ruler. He subsequently drowned himself out of despair.

2. The "three transformations" refers to the transformation of agriculture, private industry, and handicrafts production.

3. The forty-articles program represented a plan for agricultural development supported by Mao. The forty articles advocated relying on agricultural production and the domestic agricultural market, rather than foreign markets, to provide the primary accumulation needed to finance China's industrialization. The articles also advocated changing the relations of production as a condition for further developing the forces of production and increasing cooperativization. The vast majority of the peasants were to increase their income through this process. Although the forty articles were shelved during 1956 and most of 1957, they became an integral part of the Great Leap Forward.

4. As Mao here indicates, a series of meetings were held from November 1958 through early 1959. At these meetings the errors of the Great Leap were criticized and efforts made to correct them. However, it was only after these errors had been criticized and corrections made that, in July 1959, the rightists launched what Mao saw as an opportunist attack on the Great Leap and the leadership who had supported it. This perception of the rightist criticisms is reflected in the titles of the two talks Mao gave at the Lushan Conference "Why Do the Right Opportunists Now Launch an Offensive?" and "Machine Guns, Mortars, and Other Things" (reflecting the antagonistic nature of the attack.)

5. The Ma Anshan Iron and Steel Constitution refers to the authoritarian constitution of the Soviet Magnitogorsk Iron and Steel Works, which the Anshan Works, China's most advanced iron and steel works, had adopted in the 1950s. This constitution remained unchallenged until 1958. During the Great Leap Forward, the "Ma-An" principles of one person in command and technology in command were challenged in a report to the central leadership.

By March 1960, with Mao's participation, a new Anshan Constitution had been written. It combined the five principles of (1) politics in command; (2) strengthening party leadership; (3) launching vigorous mass movements; (4) instituting the "two participations, one reform, and three combinations" (cadre participation in productive labor and worker participation in management; reform of irrational and outdated rules; cooperation be-

tween workers, cadres, and technicians); and (5) go full speed ahead with technical innovations and the technical revolution. Although Mao authorized the issue, publication, and implementation of the new Anshan Constitution in March 1960, it was not until the Cultural Revolution that it was publicized in a big way.
6. A catty is 1.1 pounds.

Concerning Economic Problems of Socialism in the USSR

1. The date for this document in the 1967 edition is 1959. The 1969 edition dates it in 1958. There was no Ch'engchou (Chengzhou) Conference in November 1959, but there was one in November 1958. The document almost certainly dates from this earlier time.
2. The wage system established in 1953 emphasized predominately short-term individual material incentives. It established an eight-grade wage point system ranging from 139 to 390 wage points per month. Similar work in different regions would receive an equal number of work points, but the value of work points varied according to regional costs of living. By 1956, the wage point system had been replaced by a wage system, but the eight-grade structure was retained.
3. Experimental fields sought to develop new and advanced techniques, such as close planting, early planting, deep ploughing, etc. If successful in increasing output, the techniques would be popularized throughout China. By increasing production and thus the total wage fund, the experimental field concept could help undermine the ideological base of the graded wage system by demonstrating that specialists could learn from the peasants.

Critique of Stalin's Economic Problems of Socialism in the USSR

1. Mao is here talking about the excessive purchase of grain at the end of 1954 and the consequent rural grain shortages in the spring of 1955. Subsequently, the quota for state purchases was reduced by 7 billion catties and tension in the countryside eased. These occurrences, however, took place in the spring of 1955, not at the end of that year, which was characterized by the continuing high tide of collectivization in China's countryside.
2. Ch'in Shih Huang Ti (Qin Shi Huangdi), the first emperor, was a king of the state of Ch'in who, between 230 and 221 B.C., con-

quered the neighboring states and unified China. Under his rule, a feudal system was established, weights and measures and coinage were standardized. The legalist philosophy was the philosophical basis of the Ch'in. The first emperor is remembered for his burning of all nonutilitarian, "subversive" literature in 213 B.C.

3. Ts'ao Ts'ao (Cao Cao) was a famous general and chancellor of the latter Han dynasty (25–220 A.D.) who played a significant role in the wars which finally toppled the Han and led to the epoch of divided empire called the three kingdoms.